NAYLER & FOLLY WOOD

Peter Bennet was born in Leek, Staffordshire, in 1942. He went as a scholarship boy to King's School Macclesfield, and then to Manchester College of Art and Design, where he was influenced by the painter Norman Adams and his wife, the poet Anna Adams. He taught in secondary and further education, including two years' work with redundant men following the closure of Consett Steel Works, and subsequently spent sixteen years as Tutor Organiser for Northumberland with the Workers' Educational Association. He gave up painting for writing in 1980 and did a part-time MA in Modern English and American Literature at Newcastle University, including a study of W.S. Graham.

He has received major awards from New Writing North and Arts Council England and been a prizewinner in the National and the Arvon International Poetry Competitions, and in the Basil Bunting Awards. His books include *Sky-Riding* (1984) from Peterloo Poets; *All the Real* (1994), *Goblin Lawn: New and Selected Poems* (2005), *The Glass Swarm* (2008) and *The Game of Bear* (2011), from Flambard Press; and *Border* (2013), *Mischief* (2018) and *Nayler & Folly Wood: New & Selected Poems* (2023) from Bloodaxe Books. *The Glass Swarm* was a Poetry Book Society Choice in 2008, and was shortlisted for the T.S. Eliot Prize. *Nayler & Folly Wood* is a Poetry Book Society Special Commendation.

He helped to organise the Morden Tower poetry readings in Newcastle in the 1980s, and lived for over thirty years in a remote cottage in Northumberland associated with the ballad-writer James Armstrong, author of 'Wild Hills o' Wannys'. He now lives next to the Tyne in North Shields.

PETER BENNET

NAYLER
& FOLLY WOOD
NEW & SELECTED POEMS

BLOODAXE BOOKS

ISBN: 978 1 78037 655 4

First published 2023 by
Bloodaxe Books Ltd,
Eastburn,
South Park,
Hexham,
Northumberland NE46 1BS.

www.bloodaxebooks.com
For further information about Bloodaxe titles
please visit our website and join our mailing list
or write to the above address for a catalogue

Supported using public funding by
ARTS COUNCIL
ENGLAND

Cover design: Neil Astley & Pamela Robertson-Pearce.

Printed in Great Britain by Bell & Bain Limited, Glasgow, Scotland, on
acid-free paper sourced from mills with FSC chain of custody certification.

for the Wilds o' Wanney
and the Morden Tower

ACKNOWLEDGEMENTS

This selection is drawn from these collections by Peter Bennet: *Sky-Riding* (Peterloo Poets, 1984), *All the Real* (Flambard Press, 1994), *The Long Pack* (Flambard Press, 2002), *Goblin Lawn: New & Selected Poems* (Flambard Press, 2005), *The Glass Swarm* (Flambard Press, 2008), *Bobby Bendick's Ride*, with drawings by Birtley Aris (Enchiridion, 2010), *The Game of Bear* (Flambard Press, 2011), *Border* (Bloodaxe Books, 2013), *Ladderedge and Cotislea* (Enchiridion, 2017) and *Mischief* (Bloodaxe Books, 2018), in addition to new poems.

Individual poems have appeared in many magazines and journals and in several anthologies, including: *In Your Own Time: The Northern Poetry Workshop Anthology*, ed. Gerry Wardle (Shoestring Press, 2012); *A Speaking Silence: Quaker Poets of Today,* ed. R.V. Bailey and Stevie Krayer (Indigo Dreams Publishing, 2013); *Land of Three Rivers: The Poetry of North-East England*, ed. Neil Astley (Bloodaxe Books, 2017) and *Hollow Palaces: An Anthology of Modern Country House Poems*, ed. Kevin Gardner and John Greening, (Liverpool University Press, 2021).

CONTENTS

Light on the Wanney Crags

Warriors they are, and veterans
of long assaults;
scabbed by plots where sheep must crouch
to fret the unforgiving grass.
Their heads are emptied out by rain, their feet
abused by pitchfork-tossing pines.
Backs to the wall of sky
and stripped to grit, except
where mist or snow can compromise
their fierce nudity:
they can do nothing but resist.

Stone-shouldered and unkindly twins:
but I have seen their stacks
turned tractable by light,
and as the peaceful clouds unwind
each blown embattled height
is touched, and taught a mystery.

Then the crags stand in accord
with all whose battles are adjourned for joy:
and those, unlike the rock, who hold it fast
against a time when they may fall
among the kindnesses of light
infrequently, or not at all.

Crazy Dog

Distance has dwindled him to running points:
his quick white dash, his smudge of black,
are accidents beneath the bulk of sky,
small movements in a weighted sack.

He risks a start, tail sprung with confidence,
but stops before a second passes,
supplicates, then tacks a reckless angle,
sheepdog-fashion, through the sheepless grasses.

There must be countless crazy ways
to be a crazy dog – shadow-poaching,
calling echoes from the moon –
this one sees the sky itself encroaching

on his liberty. The failing daylight strikes
no barriers which are not his alone:
a dog with half the world to run across,
who acts as though somebody pegged him down.

He'll find the road eventually, or else
his owners at their summer caravan
will stir themselves to fetch him home,
and lock him up so he feels free again.

The Silence

(for Rosa Davis)

Traces can be found towards the lough
and soon I hold
a full-grown silence in my sights:

a lack of sound more elderly and grand
than all the pines and birches
whose water-edge I share. It rests

across the lap of water like a blade,
separating trees and sky
from their reflecting selves. Perhaps

my bench of driftwood cracks: the silence
listens, turns and starts.
The geese are up and walk towards me,

shorewards on a plank of light: clumsily
they raise unruly wings,
breaking out their syllables like hounds.

Lottie Little and the Trees

Imagine her thin sticks up there –
Lottie Little – while she doled
her soup of rue and solitude
and slouched trees spat into the bowl.

Outside, the fell's cold vacancy
and inside, that intention rooting
deeper as each year drew in
to have them hacked and burned to nothing.

Imagine the elder by the gate –
which once purled sunlight to entangle
the taste of milk with greenery
for children grown while she stayed single –

cut down for what she heard it murmur.
And even then she could remember.

Souvenir of Malling

The iron-corseted Moselle,
in black, with bands of chilly light;
a burp and swash of barge-trains running
cargo out from Germany;
an onion-turret fussed by trees.

Although a year churns in between
that dawn and this, the goldcrest wren –
brisk, thrilling smallness, now, this morning,
flanked by ferns like greater wings –
can flit my distance to all these.

My son, reached soonest, among reeds,
as engines clubbing hard at water
fractured sleep and drew us down
to count the wealth, in shrouded tons,
dark with dew from Germany.

And turned me, not to have him share
my fear of strong means, dimly seen,
by which unwieldy laden hulls
slide through nights unceasingly,
like fathers following their sons.

Síle na Gig or Playmate of the Month

I met her on a freezing morning
where the road clings to the lough.
She made three beckonings:
from a cow-pat near my feet to start with,
merely lifting amber knees,
the hardly-there-at-all chemise,
and sharpening her grin.

Farther on, between two heather-brakes,
naked this time, smudged by light,
the same insistent glossy shape,
each hand weighing out a breast,
nipples pertinently pricked,
hair in an entanglement,
elsewhere a tuft, her covert lip.

I turned for home, and there among the sheep
she sat again, attracting me
by shifting slightly in the wind.
She made her wide split-beaver, ancient M,
a finger at the opened curls:
held me, the only moorland beast
equipped to read her, stupidly enthralled.

Barmaid

Floundering in her pool of faces,
with scarcely chance to scratch an itch,
she dips her head, gulps privacy,
bobs among the pin-up bitches'

buoyant bubs, as pink as scampi,
which bring strange fishes looming down.
Glances like the lips of lampreys
are lifting flesh on all her bones.

Despite her aches she twirls to serve
but thoughtlessly displays a thigh.
In frothy swirls the blunt snouts swerve
and every glass contains an eye.

Funny Man

Good-looking, gloomy, awkward cuss:
he'd never dance.
But let somebody ask his wife...
You'd have some action from him then,
as edgy as a chisel-bag.

It was the fall that sorted him,
the whole height of the foundry crane:
surgery, six months in plaster,
surgery again.
Great pain unlocked a funny man,
and when they came to wheel him home
he'd salvaged laughs from splintered bone
and friends for every foot he fell.

He sees the bright side nowadays:
finds life too short.
And dance? He'll get up when you like,
three-legged if you count the stick,
and twitch his boots and callipers.

Looking Through a Parched Sea Holly Bush

I see three things that bring me grief:
first, among the cross-toothed curls,
two pearly snails
anchored to a drying leaf;

then, how heat-clasped boulders sit,
each old when some first living thing
woke up to its journeying,
rubbing down again to grit;

and, farther out than I can reach,
how woman-like my daughter wades,
careless that her girlhood fades,
as sea takes home the sun-warmed beach.

Fête Day at Bellingham

I

Prevarication among coals:
the darkness loiters,

lichen grips a thousand stones
each offered, quiet as a pulse.

Morning stalls, delays
acceptance of a moorland shape.

Curlews questioned me from sleep
to pass on news of this:

my hearth's assertion of a flame
and daylight, dragged on with my clothes.

II

Sun has saddled up the square
and rides to music

shovelled from a drop-side truck.
Livestock gathers limp rosettes and stares

past oddment stalls and fancy dress
to where the river slackens speed

and tadpole parliaments
debate a subtlety of tiny points.

But we have chosen kerbside vetch
and blue-as-beetroot columbines.

III

Simplified by dusk
we lock our door

on darkness and a sheep-wracked hill.
Closeness joins us at the edge of sleep

and urgency, until dismissed to picnic-fields
where doves combine in crimson blooms

or villages
where suns as delicate as scythes

turn cartwheels in a hive of streets
and interlock their eyes.

Not at Home

(for Richard Kell)

You ask for poems built like walls
against the infiltrating frost, the purple
storms of rhetoric.

I'd choose windows, craftily reflecting
each Peeping Tom.

But strong walls crumple,
and glass melts into scorching tears,
as soon as I move closer and peer through
to that small room
Erato and Calliope share –
the broken stylus and the rickety lyre,
and all that mail on the mat.

Hareshaw Linn

is inching nearer
its beginning.

However hard its teeth are gritted,
stone is bitten. Water fumes,
squeezed by its entourage of oak, of beech –
earth lifter, rummaging in spate.

Among this crockery of cliffs,
outriding trees
have dangled wishbones of their dead
like timber lightning.
Resentful of your footsteps, they
discharge, through loopholes in the rock,
their weaponry
in bursts of rooks.

There's no way home
except the route you got here by.

Go back.

High moorland has been scoured for snow,
the melt
leans forward in an upright thunder.

Sandstone pressure
bends rainbows to the neck of water.

Winter Hills

Beyond the lichened balustrade, I saw
my parents on a shelving lawn,
one Saturday, the start of summer.

Though men cut timber in the higher woods,
and children squawked from shrubberies,
a twang of insects dulled each sound.

He wore his khaki, she the soft print dress
that's famous in the photographs –
they glanced towards me joyfully, and smiled.

But I am not the one that they remembered,
and only I can see the birches bend
across the slope where they embraced each other,

and how the winter hills close round.

Duddo Stones

(for my wife)

Summer grips us in its damp
grey palm. But there, across a quarter-mile
of perfect wheat, are blinks of sunlight choosing,
one by one, grooved faces of five megaliths
to celebrate, beyond the wind-stroked crop
that balks us, and by balking speaks
for stones whose prime contemporary role
is surely the dumb oracle.

We'll hike back here at harvest time
to put more closely what it is
we can't quite ask,
and meanwhile leave, beside untrodden wheat,
a miserly libation
of lukewarm coffee from a Thermos flask.

Face Painting at Threpwood Hill

(for Linda France)

This child will not be the first
to dream his parents in a garden,
young and smiling, fond and close,
standing as they are before him.

Wind churns gouts of elder blossom,
tosses just the kind of salad
Eden was. Land curls its pages
like Genesis towards the Tyne,
that forked tongue snaking to the sea.

Half-afraid to be the beast
squiggles on his face have made him,
he threatens through a mask of smears
to eat the world, including them.

He will, and after comes the dream.

First Calf

(for Maggie Bede)

1

No pasture yet, a threshing floor
where wind beats chaff

from skittered snow. A half-light, spinning,
finds but will not warm at all

her blunt head,
levelled like a ram,

stretch-mouthed for an aria.
From bagpipe on her four black legs, the first

calf of the year is dropping,
swaddled into blood, but dying.

2

Stumble-foot, man snatches rope –
the dragged scrap makes for simple drawing,

zigzag on the fellside slope,
a fragile trace

which solemnly treads out to nothing.
Every step the mother, licking,

calls full-throated in the hush
of storm blown inside out. The sky

is veined like afterbirth, too wide and red
for such a meagre tragedy.

At the Queen's Hall

(for John Harle)

As silent as a catafalque,
the grand piano points its toes,
demurely underpinning bulk.

A mourner (sorry) pianist
and pageboy, tallow-blond and mute,
likewise extend their toes and wrists

towards their hope, the hierophant,
assured (if even art decays)
that one soprano saxophone

will blow the furnace doors, and blaze.

The Old Moor House

To navigate, the top clump of a scoured copse,
accoustic, when the wind allows
for twitterings –
just now, incorrigible hush.

The haunted inn is farther still,
good stone not quite tottering,
a roofless reticence preserved
in nettle smell.

They couldn't stop the murders here, despite
a gibbet opposite the door.

But there's no fright from what persists.

That hoof fall and that snort of breath
are just a thin girl on a white-faced pony,
leading another, riderless.

Cancer Patient

Prune them hard, she says,
her treatment over,
advising me on raspberries.

I think instead
back to my opposite of gardens –
railway cuttings
scorched the height of their steep sides
and sometimes wild raspberries,
smouldering in their coils like fuses,
contriving green.

Extraction

Houses, like teeth,
seem bigger than the space they occupy.

They hold so much
love, for instance, and its slow goodbye,
then leave no Where at all,
a blank
for dock and rosebay willowherb.

And both can still be visited.

I tongue the dimple in my gum –
a little well
that offers me my blood for tasting,
out of pity for myself.

Logan Street

(for Anne Stevenson)

The hearth's a chatterbox. Wind slouches,
eavesdropping, borrowing a voice.
Floorboards concur. The walls are itching
beneath their plaster to converse.

You offered all there is of welcome
to this house at the point of speech. I'm mooching
at home among your rooms, your books. My thumb
is loosening the tongues of latches.

The Murrough Lady

1

Please do not ask him
to describe her body, he
did not look back again, perhaps
afraid to try.

That is his tragedy,
for very few have seen
her step free from her ground and weather,
her apple-green.

The world she wore
is strewn about him, nonetheless,
as he approximates her shape
with fetishes.

2

So tall the sleet clouds
rode with her, and wind
brought something of her voice within it, we
were scavenging her property –
at her arrival,
cringed like yard dogs, felt
her brisk blows quench our quarrelling
and better so.

Such bones we squabbled for
were muddied up past nourishing –

such shrill disputes
were each one's shrill cries echoing.

She spoke to us
as silence does, to underlife
which could recall the simple speech,
and make some glottal recess twitch
to murmur, *Mistress, welcome home.*

Driving off the eager,
chose the strong,
awarding manhood in her way.

Widow of so many friends,
she overleans my arm,
resorts to rain as though to tears
for idle ground,
the tilth of which she must maintain.

If I accept her subtle life,
my bargain will be not to ask
the world prismatic,
knowledge striding like the light,
or money-love or woman-love,
but tenancy of rising fields.

And when the season tilts
on end, no share
of harvest,
but freedom of her inner rooms,
the muckyards and the granaries
of her imaginary farms.

Time taps my heart impatiently,
but she is girlish, without age,

far richer than we had supposed,
haughty always, cruel at the harnessing.

The bargain was agreed, perhaps.
I can remember
only the stink of breaking earth, the sting,
the ribbed yoke of her heavy plough.

Each night a half-sleep,
never waking
to reap the brightness and the singing.

   3

We harnessed darkness
to our need.
Of all unpleasant duties there,
I most disliked
to pour the rivulets of gory bait
and listen
for slobbering among the traps.

Such hard work, killing, even so,
her grave stayed empty but for seepage. Those
detailed to bury her returned
with rigmaroles
of windings left on hurdles, or
her body woken in miasma.
Our great fires singularly failed.

I shivered through the ritual.
Sometimes we heard
echoes of her hungry calling
entangling our manly shout.
But fear is not appropriate. Her build
is smaller, largely, than our own.
Often she seemed beautiful.

Berenson at the Borghese

(for Dominic)

His beard is frosted eagerness,
whiter than the panama
so neatly garnished with a ribbon
black as his suit
among the shadows thrown by art.

Informed by light, and yet his eyes
seem bruised by seeing.

The odalisque
is languor and solidity –
her chevelure like coral at the nape,
her long back sinking,
rising almost,
across a marble ottoman.

His gaze is labour –
she is shiftless, splendidly
uninterested in her beauty.

Her age extends
beyond the age of stone or making.

At ninety, Berenson distils
the taste of Europe in his looking.

The Exhibition of the Esquimaux

at the Hull Maritime Museum

In a sea of dark clothes, walrus faces
close in towards the makeshift gravel beach
where Uckaluk has stocked her mother's grave
with ingenuities in bone and stitched
hide which are her only history. She kneels
as though to die among her dogs
in plain view of a British whaler.

Ice and piety are inching nearer.
She is fifteen this winter and so scrawny
her limbs are thin as baleen. Captain Parker
will not weigh anchor with a single woman
so Memiadluk is chosen and the couple
are educated, cleansed and married,
aboard the *Truelove* out of Hull.

When shown in Northern towns, the honeymooners
capture all hearts with their docility
and gratitude. *They are Raw Meat Eaters,*
Surgeon Gedney's handbill states, their Form is not
dissimilar to that of the Quadroon,
but note that, like the Hottentot,
they have a Mild and Sad Expression.

These beneficiaries of British Rule subsist
only by charity of Whaling Vessels.
Yet even they, supplied with Shot and Muskets,
might feed themselves and, furthermore, establish
by Trade in Hides and Oils of Seal and Whale
such Commerce as would march abreast
with Propagation of the Gospel.

Captain my father now, Surgeon my mother...
Twelve thousand walruses each paid one shilling
to hear her utter, and to see her consort
pose in his kayak with a spear. Real weather
whitens the arctic backdrop and time fades
their image like an oleograph
above the mantelpiece of trade.

Le Plan des Pennes

(for Margaret and François)

1

Up at the ancient settlement
it's hot white limestone gripping tinder,
Roman cart ruts and cigalles.

A mountain toothache lowers
a Boeing 737 towards
the wrecked cars and the quarries
round L'Estaque, against the light.

The airport is a tyre-smirched springboard
out into L'Étang de Berre,
it bounces grace,
stills a pirouette to jetsam.

Futures in a fan of cards
are peddled at the café tables.

The gendarme knows the gypsy's past,
her future also.

2

Pas là, not there –
though M. Pala isn't here,
his stud boar is.

Its pen is small, its penis big.

Bulk and stink are factual, its eyes
are roving, sailor blue.

Tomorrow it escapes. Me too.

A little glare shaped like a trotter
waits on the pavement for my foot
to step on, into gold, below
the window of the restaurant
high in the Basilica de Saint-Victor
where a waiter offers to his sea, his city,
all the songs he has for nothing.

M. Pala flogs his pig
back from the village to its snout-deep wallow.

Pas là, not there –
he flogs himself
from cash to shit and back again,
no wiser.

3

Pleases and thankyous fill the crypt
like candles, like a shoal of crutches,
like model aeroplanes, like boats, like flowers
choked in cellophane.

Pas là, not there –
Christ's body is a waxy sprawl
islanded in candlelight,
a paper rose
pressed into the deepest wound.

THE LONG PACK

I tremble to tell you! We are all gone,
for it is a living pack.

JAMES HOGG

Northumberland is a rough county.

SIR NIKOLAUS PEVSNER

I

Darkness is my second mother,
the pack a double blindness, in whose caul
I must not move,
but grip my butcher's knife, my silver whistle,
and wait till silence matches dark,
to cut free like a savage child.

I am about my act, my strange acte,
my worke, my strange work.

II

Now Bellingham is briefly hers.

The oiled gate
is quiet as a book to open.

Inside, the yew tree is a flame's
dark opposite,
smudged upon the inner eye,
it struggles upward, angled to its stem,
and cannot leave the ground.

My stone's a lid on grass,
but mind is calling me to mind, as if
I might be here awake and answering
bones above the layered bones.

The iron latch-tail chills,
and clings to moisture on her palm.

I'm seeing what I don't remember,
and so are you, imagining my fear,
and sacking chafing at my face.

I breathe stale merchandise,
and, as a lantern flares through cloth,
embrace a tremor in the air.

Whosoever hears of it,
both his ears shall tingle.

III

At sunset, Midas fished the Tyne,
or else the gentry of Northumberland
are melting all their riches down.

Gold slides past kingcups to the sea,
but here, where common boulders sit,
colours are of coal and lead.

My father stumbles from the flow:
his hands are empty, but his head
has feasted on philosophy.

That man he countless times heard preach
against the rule and stink of priests maintained,
one Lord's day sixty years ago,
he met God walking in an open field,
to his eyes seeming strange,
a man deformed, clad in patched clouts.

God looked wishly on him, and he pittied God.

The Tyne would bubble like a sore
if it absorbed
the rage my father steeps in it.

Our supper slips to deeper water.

IV

Time rattles in the ewe's throat.

Mist blots up stories from the fell,
muffles moorland industry, conceals
herd and soldier, park and steading,
tumulus and battlestone,
the horse that bolted with the bride,
lots drawn, stratagems forgotten.

The dead do not know who they are
until they are remembered.

V

A fly strums glass,
and bumps the distances your window holds.

Blue hills, remembering to be
Roxburghshire, across the Border,
stand for all that's torn away,
like Houxty Wood:
the nymphs lamenting for their dear resort.

The fly is stitching
shreds of history to hills,
and patching nearer times with fields.

The past lies in the sun beyond the pane.

Art poor? Yea, very poor, said He.

VI

At Warden, where the two Tynes meet
behind my father's empty hands,
I see the solemn water break
into a curve of countless brilliants
across my memory, as rich and starry
as Colonel Ridley's chandeliers,
and one great salmon in their midst
stand upon its tail for ever.

This is a true story, most true in the history.

The fish is one of diverse signs
that comfort me
in this concealment where I am
still visible,
if you will please imagine it.

The plague of God is in your purses,
did you not see my hand stretched out?

VII

She thumbs an apple in her pocket
and somewhere thunder scrapes a drum.

The fieldgate jigs,
its wreckage flouncing baler-twine.

Sunlight on a shattered gable
hints at past prosperity:
The Orchard on its tidy portion.

Drystone dikes beside the path
rise again among the nettles,
and deeply fumbling ruts reveal

the old highroad across the Rede,
broad enough for carts to pass, or haul
harvest towers, two abreast.

Tyme tryeth Troth.

Her apple pleases
a roan mare by the broken barn.

VIII

The Jacobite rose-bush
strikes your wall with small, white blossoms.

Fallen petals sign the ground:
Derwentwater, Forster, Mad Jack Hall.

Northumberland is Arcady.

The paperback you've pushed aside
has Radcliffe an Initiate,
the rose a mystery
bred by the Prieuré de Sion.

IX

It is meat and drink to an Angel
to swear a full-mouthed oath.

The deeds and discourse
of that great engine of disorder, Richard Last,
so pressed my father's waxy spirit
that two-score years of witnessing
and sundry buffetings we all and each endured
have not ground smooth their stamp.

Neither the death of Mr Last
in this world, or the dissolution
of his lewd company,
nor yet the ruination of our farm,
the self-same Orchard, could abate
his whistling multifarious fancies.

My deer ones consider,
here is no lodging, no safe habitation.

X

Lord of the wood was my game once:
Rob o' Risingham and Robin Hood,
the king within the oak in summer time.

The Oak-Leaves me embroyder all,
between them Caterpillars crawl
and Ivy, with familiar trails,
me licks, and clasps, and curls, and hales.

A boy's face, smiling among leaves,
tells me I shall live again.

XI

To be alone is always new.

Outside your window, past the rosebush
and the garden, moorland pasture
steeps its skirts in the arriving night.

Booze turns the landscape into art.

Cloudscapes you have watched since noon
are smouldering and charged with thunder,

while fells regroup as gloomy leas
and boskage: school of Claude Lorraine.

Pools and streams snag threads of light
in jagged valleys and defiles.

Above Greenrigg, a crabwise track
climbs gothic heights
towards a crumbling tower of cumulus.

You see a well, which sad trees overhang,
and flame and woodsmoke by a ruined arch,
or in some bouldered clearing,
and, always there, the same two countrymen
in ragged costume of their age.

The elder stoops to coax the fire, the younger
leans forward on his staff. Sometimes
they picturesquely fish a stream
or crouch as if in hope beside the path.

I am found of those that sought me not.

XII

The Karrimor rucksack biffs the ground
and stillness
steps into the air behind her.

The weight she cannot feel but as a pulse
of unexpected modesty
is only our attention resting
beside her in the holly garden.

Tasselled nettles, ivy with its frog-shaped leaves,
are seeking what they most resemble.

Solvitur ambulando.

Drops of water on the leaves of holly
remind her of fragility:
but all at once the hopelessness
her erstwhile husband, Dr Pordage, calls
'a little seasonal depression'
seems light enough for all such surfaces.

In Jesmond, her thesis on the pastoral mode
awaits completion
in black bin-liners by a makeshift desk.

XIII

Come, let us goe, while we are in our prime,
and take the harmless follie of the time.

Our one flesh, Marjorie,
that was a chandler's wife at Hexham,
had pissed my mother's bed in drink
the night they put me to her.

Last and my father preached extempore
and my flesh rose.

What God has cleansed, call thou not uncleane.

XIV

With little interruption by its islands,
the Indian Ocean
vastly folds and smooths its rigs.

Beach fires of the heathen raise
a level smoke veil
that separates the sea-flats and the bastion,
and laden barges from the masts at anchor.

Within a cannon-shot of Fort St George,
a resting ox looks up at whip crack,
another, and a distant cry,
to witness English law enacted.

My father ploughed with oxen still
the cloud-swabbed slope below The Orchard,
before the sheep came everywhere
and Richard Last began to preach and print
the blood that crieth in the ears.

His rigs are there for evening sun to notice
as if a grassy main had clenched
the farm, and that become a wrecked stone ship,
its cargo sunk into the moor.

The sea forgives the keel its furrow.

XV

The treasure came to port at London,
and then aboard a collier vessel
pertaining to Sir William Blackett, Baronet,
and then by cart from Newcastle.

That, I myself was witness to.

There is a little sparke lies under
thine honour, pomp and riches,
which shall consume, as it is written.

XVI

Howl, howl, ye nobles, howl honourable,
for the miseries that come upon you.

Is your face towards the light?

Even a tendril of the rose-bush
the night wind stirs against your wall
will leave a groove an axe might cut.

Together, remember, we have cauled
the youth I was
in darkness and a pedlar's pack,
while time in Lee Hall kitchen ticks
three hundred years
against the measure of my heart.

Are you in trembling of a rich man's clock?

Consider the spine of one great tree,
its branches lopped, its saw cut vertebrae
tumbled into English grass.

For our parts, wee'l have all things common,
wee'l break our bread from house to house.

XVII

The housemaid's whisper frightens me.

Come, our wanderer is a shepherdess
whose thoughts are grazing
in sunlit parkland, where a fine grey house
stands back politely,
paid-for out of coal and lead.

Passion plucks no berries
from the myrtle and ivy
nor calls upon Arethuse and Mincius,
nor tells of rough satyrs, and fauns
with cloven heel...

Trim nails against the texture of her page
prevent a breeze from turning it.

Is this thy love, thy dove, thy fair one?

Consoling emblems slip my mind,
and she has closed her eyes to see them:
the salmon in its pelt of light,
the treasure cart,
and then the very last I saw
before tarred cloth enveloped me,
a white bull, motionless
against the gathered and substantial dark
of Houxty Wood,
and the moon and stars in ecstasy.

I must not move.

XVIII

Claude's pictures fade, and leave your window
locked darkly on Northumberland.

Chesterhope's a muddy doormat:
you are a poem-spider trod thereon.

What have we then? A revelation?
Or normal untruth soaking bones
of whinstone in a bleating mist?

There's more to pastoral than meets the eye.

XIX

My honeymoon left me a widower:
a mourner at an empty grave, moreover,
and still the priest to pay.

As high of heart as she would ride of old,
Helen, who that wild day in death's despite
escaped the durance of the churchyard mould.

Thus I have also known despair.

XX

How will you meet her, by the way?

She reads the papers. You could try,
sincere male wishes (ho ho)
for friendship and outings (ha ha).

No no.

Be wise now therefore. O ye Rulers
be instructed. Give over, give over
thy midnight mischief.

A chance encounter might be engineered.

A pilgrimage to see the Templars' mark
where Derwentwater's brother, of the Prieuré,
may pensively have placed his fingers.

You could share that.

A sound like rain across the dry church roof,
or one short cry from empty shrubbery,
might get you talking in that haunted place.

XXI

This is your summer, and the oak tree
grips its leaves about my face.

The last Leveller that was shot to death:
a face of leaves
that stares back smiling at your own.

It took five tons of oak to smelt one ton
of iron, a skelp of land to feed one sheep.

For you, we ranting Angels might have turned
oak roots in the wards of earth
to unlock England for her cheated yeomanry.

The very shadow frighted you
and shook your kingdome.

Rout out the titled man in every hollow,
unfurling park land, dunning for his rents!

The substantiality of levelling is comming.

XXII

Sinne and transgression is finisht,
a meere riddle, that they
with all their humane learning cannot reade.

North Tyne, untarnished by the moon, I see
still flows stealthily by Houxty. A shield
of pasture there may yet contain
the like of that heraldic bull
whose glimmering stillness strengthened me, the night
we wove our stratagem within the wood.

Alan, that was my lost bride Helen's brother,
my father, busy as a gnat,
poor drunken Marjorie: their divers ends
I cannot know. Together with myself,
whose death you must be privy to,
this was our one flesh dwindled to its remnant.

Some beer, some scraps of bread and meat, a sword,
two knives, and one great pistol
my father brandished like the cuddy's jawbone
Samson hefted, owning neither shot nor powder:
these, with my silver whistle and a Bible,
comprised our final commonwealth.

Thou and thy Family are fed,
as the young ravens strangely.

XXIII

Then, since we mortal lovers are,
ask not how long our love will last;
but while it does, let us take care
each minute be with pleasure passed.

Her boots and anorak
are in the kitchen with a residue
of spaghetti carbonara, cheese and apples,
and Côtes du Roussillon Villages.

She's heard of Rennes le Château and the Prieuré,
and shares your view
across Greenrigg to Derwentwater's stone
and light withdrawing.

I see that she herself removes,
after her dungarees and Oxfam jumper,

surprisingly upmarket underwear
and helps you slip into the grateful place
last occupied by Dr Pordage.

Did Daphnis and his nymph, or Danaë
beneath her shower of gold enjoy
such raptures in Arcadia?

XXIV

Twigs drawn in half-dark from my father's fist
decide our parts: Alan shall play
the stout cajoling pedlar, I, with fierce
and silent eloquence, his burden.

We have, of rope and canvas taken
by stealth from Marjorie's chandler's yard,
sufficiency, though it be foul.

Lee Hall is Troy, its garrison
a housemaid and a gardener
who wags a blunderbuss named Copenhagen.

Deliver, deliver,
my money that thou hast to rogues,
whores and cut-purses, who are flesh of thy flesh,
or els by my selfe, saith the Lord,
I will torment thee day and night.

Colonel Ridley's heathen treasure
will buy us passage to America
and land for freeborn Angels to rejoice in.

An unkind wind
strews silver on the river's velvet
counter like a money lender.

XXV

Give over thy base and stinking formall grace
before and after meat, give over
thy nasty, stinking family duties,
thy Gospell Ordinances;
for under them lies snarling, snapping,
biting, covetousnesse, evill surmising,
envy, malice, and horrid hypocrisie.

Give over, or if nothing els will do it,
I'l make thy child, in whom thy soul delighted,
lie with a whore before thine eyes.

By that base thing, that plaguy holinesse
and righteousnesse of thine shall be confounded,
and thou plagued back, damned and rammed
into thy mother's womb that is Eternity.

Then thou shall see no evill furthermore
but rather one huge beauty,
but first lose righteousness and holinesse
and every crum of thy Religion.

XXVI

Your duck-down duvet jerks and slides.

Now I can address you both. Outside,
thin snow sheets a whinstone bed.

Is my borrowed voice too faint? Too loud?

I fear I am no better hand
at haunting than at levelling:
beneath my slab, a bone-cache

tangled in the yew tree's roots,
I wait for recognition and for naming
while witnessing my own conception.

Ther's my riddle.

My hinny in her poor bunched shroud,
thrown from the lathered back of Heatherbell,
had the swan-begotten queen for namesake,
and yet still waits for burial
unless a mine or hag received her.

I know that beasts more easily return,
their souls more apt,
as Heatherbell the roan came back
to haunt The Orchard for the apple
your new love gave her.

Feare thou not,
creep forth a little in this mystery.

XXVII

Time rattles in the ewe's throat
and time would faile if I would tell you all.

I saw diversity, variety, distinction
and as clearly saw
all folded into Unity,
and that has been my song since then.

The dead do not know who they are
until they are remembered.

XXVIII

She steps towards me in the early morning.

A lantern flares, and Copenhagen utters
the word that lifts me
above the stink of my own blood.

My cloth womb splits.

In Houxty Wood,
mist turns to smallest rain to make
visible a shift of air
that tilts the faces of the leaves.

She kneels, unwary
as she quickens, finding pipe-ash lichen,
oyster lichen, tiny rubies
delightful on my narrow stone.

It was thus resembled,
as if a great brush dipt in whiting
should sweep a picture off a wall.

The voice you hear has made itself your child.

Ha-Ha

Let me affirm that what I have not done
remains a plant so valueless
that I have never learned its shape or name.

It thrives, a clump of uncommitted spirit,
between me and the *saut-de-loup*, or *ha-ha*.

It was in Paris, or on the Riviera,
entre deux guerres, for sure, that someone
quite unknown to me, but close,
had picked a bunch, and tied it with a ribbon,
to throw into a grave I will not enter.

Spalpeen

Time's up for you inside my myth,
so shout at every turning of the tune,
and clap your hands
to have this moment for your pleasure.

Fact steps forward to reveal you,
clean-shaven, and of medium height,
like every spalpeen in the land.

Outside, trams flash and clang
through Celtic twilight, and the rain
that slicks the courtyard of the School of Art
shines the stone limbs of Cuchulain,
the lord of skirmish and unlucky frolic.

You gave me nothing but permission.

I was your shadow, and my dumb attention
a story harped on long ago
which made for grief, just as the love
of my fair rival, Kathleen of the duffel coat,
led towards the lake of weeping.

Tithonus at Kielder

Since death avoids you, every longed-for morning
hurts worse than death, and evenings turn
from grey to purple without hope.

Cheer up, old grasshopper, at least
you had the guts to claim the dawn
before the hours indignant worked their wills.

The woods decay and fall, so fell
and plant again, and celebrate your days
as if they danced like sunlit leaves
caught in the backstream of a timber waggon
returning on its silver wheels.

Fairytale

The children dream a foray, and their bodies
follow on their hands and knees
out from the forest, under barbed wire fences.

The wind among the trees is scolding.

A company of white geese by the stream,
down where the lane goes through a farmyard
overhung and dark with oaks,
are moonlit so that they resemble
excisions from an older, radiant world.

These are dream geese, docile, and too beautiful
to raise their wings in clamour, or to scatter.

Breath keeps pace as bare soles, gladdening
to soft damp earth and smell of prey,
accelerate a measured run,
and this is good, and this is human nature.

Wolf-girls, wolf-boys, spread your arms
find balance, vocalise your hunger.

Each night the geese are there again, but stronger.

The Fossil

She knows that it is risky, nowadays,
woken by chance and in the dark,
not to keep herself in focus.

Last night she had been slithering
back into the quarry basin,
the thick green water and the jewelled silt.

She thinks of people and professions
there to help her, in their fashion.

She thinks of sweet, unconscious preservation
in sediment, her life a gem
of which she only knows the special virtue.

Is she a bat-like thing? A hippogriff?

The self she had not thought she could remember
has left a path to be completed.

She sees again, in landscape squeezed of light,
her early footprints, each claw perfect,
blurring, then in turn unblurring,
in thin dust drifting at the quarry's rim.

The Damp Harmonium

The sea is cold, the moon is veiled,
and clouds are frantic with the coming storm.

A salt-bleached stile leads down to where
the graveyard is, and milky foam
embroiders rocks, as rising swell
attacks the shore and falls back, breaking.

Tonight a ship must surely founder.

The only craftsman on the island
has cut down every tree there was,
and now he is reduced to driftwood
to make his souvenirs and toys
and all the coffins in his workshop.

It's true that here we see the world
as if it were a long way off
until the ocean brings it closer.

The village hall is furnished as a chapel:
the minister has long departed
and yet his congregation comes
unsummoned at the hour of worship.

The storm breaks and the lamps grow dim.

See how the drowned have filled the doorway,
incandescent in their youth and beauty,
and how the damp harmonium is gleeful.

Please stand and join us as we raise our voices
to sing the island's only hymn.

The Pigeon Loft

No doubt you will have heard of his remark
that firelight on a darkened window
resembled all that seemed to stand
between him and the fecund, various world
from out of which his powers came.

He was adept at obfuscation.

He also may have said that music flies
into the ears on small black wings:
but attribution there is shaky.

Somehow, during his sojourn in Prague,
he found material for those delusions
for which his short career is now remembered.

We are unlikely to discover,
behind the smoke-clouds and dark instruments,
where exactly research led him,
or what he let loose in the pigeon loft.

He earned a bonfire for himself, that's clear
if you examine the aghast expression
he wears in that last woodcut, or the knock-
kneed verses of his *True Confession*.

Squiffy

This trek has been like never learning,
with every step the same mistake,
and something vital left behind
among the trees, down where the fever swarms
vibrate beneath the heavy leaves.

What he's been looking for is there, abruptly,
and then the mountain elbows out the view.

Yes, there it is again, the shimmering house,
with its verandah in a wedge of dark,
tethered to its track out from the bush.

There is no sign of cooking-smoke, or cattle,
no dog is barking in the stable-yard.

The air is still, the midday light impartial.

It's time for him to start the long descent
towards the camp-bed in the shade, the gramophone.

It's strange how one idea sticks in his head.

It's nothing, really, only a daftness:
like the chap who once, back home, got squiffy
and fought a goblin on the vicar's lawn.

Breathe Carefully

In your attic there could be a shrouded globe,
some tinsel, flashbulbs, and a picture book.

If not, some bobbins and a rocking horse,
or, better still, an old piano stool,
a dusty window, and a dying moth:
it doesn't matter, work with what you find,
so long as you have all you need for stitching.

When you see the man-shape and its shadow,
look right through them, make the voice of thunder.

The job, of course, must not remain too solid.

Peel off one dimension, make it flat
enough to slide the whole thing sideways
into the future of your certain person,
precisely when he turns away abruptly,
dismissing you, and is not mindful
of your importance, his fragility.

If this seems difficult, go back
and practise basic wrapping and unfolding.

Nothing is achieved without expenditure:
before you start, try emptying your purse
into an unfamiliar ditch or culvert
while snow falls, and the beggars are in shelter.

Breathe carefully, a little at a time,
unhook the phone, and bolt your door.

The Imp

Watch how you go, the path down there
is blocked in parts by builders' rubble,
and slippy under rotting leaves.

The house is cramped but neat, and both
the parents of the imp are solid folk,
the father clever with his hands, the mother
not knowing how to let herself be idle.

Encourage them in conversation.

They will speak proudly of its horns and tail
and rough skin, caustic to the touch.

I'll be astonished if you fail
to find the fixity of their devotion
comforting, in some ways, to the mind.

If you intend to make a close inspection,
present my compliments, and take
your gardening gloves and overalls,
and something for the lad himself, perhaps
a horseshoe for a teething-ring.

The Sally Garden

Become a puppy once again
and leave your half-chewed catalogue
of wasted chances on the rug
of snug regrets and snuff the sweet
night air among the sally trees.

Gaps in the stonework of the wall, and ivy
entangled in the trellises,
seem etched by moonlight to provide
good lodgements for your teeth and paws.

I see you also now have hands and toes.

Once up, reach for the sally boughs and tug
yourself towards me while I set your feet
upon the stone head of Mnemosyne.

She's mossy, but securely placed
for you to slither down, into the fog
of what was once a paradise.

Let's see no sadness in your eyes.

I have arranged some things of yours
together in a single thought:
an awful childhood and a spade
left in the ground to rust, and scars
of earth amid the wilderness,
as if someone with half a mind
to find a good spot for a grave had dug
without conviction, or a dog
had half remembered where a bone was laid.

The Angel

The snow is feather-like and slow descending
between the spires, and now the room
itself begins to fill with feathers
that glow and give off sounds and odours.

Put down your notebook: pass the lamp.

This is an outcome we must spare
no time or labour to suppress.

Up through the neck comes speech, the damp
core only of each vocable,
and then that diffident, sweet-natured smile
returns as if it can remember,
each time it tries to lift a wing
from off the rag rug by the study fire,
the outspread heavens, like a curtain.

Our colleagues will endorse our course of action.

This creature is too frail to bear –
pull back my shirt cuffs if you will, Professor –
our human narrowness of range and know
each hour it lives that it must die,
and meanwhile drag its feet through slush, and never
ascend in splendour into falling snow.

JIGGER NODS

Warner, whose immortal pen
praised every honest Englishman
that strives to set old Albion free
from giants of adversity,
founded our school and built our rule
in good Queen Bess's reign.

The Founder's Anthem

We think no greater blisse than such
to be as be we would,
when blessèd none but such as be
the same as be they should.

WILLIAM WARNER, *Albion's England*

I

Is it still visible, the bright
imaginary green,
within this future we are moving to?

Jigger sees it, all a dazzle,
beyond the monkeypuzzle tree.

II

Wind, time, and sun reel shadows back
to flicker over market stalls
towards the coke-works and the shunting yard,
a greasy café wedged beneath an arch,
and hinterland where sooty hills are dozing.

There, in that town, are the fleet of foot,
the armoured and the many-headed.

Stables brim and reek, a thousand
inky essays wait for marking,
and amazons rebuff him, one by one,
except Hippolytë, who leaves
her girdle on the field of battle.

Ex pede Herculem!

The world is worse than it was then,
thinks Jigger, with a crooked troupe
of immigrants and nancy-boys
exploiting Albion, and grinding down
the spirit of her Englishmen.

III

For many years he livèd thus,
stipended so to live,
and shepherd-like to teach a flock
himself did wholly give...

Put your feet up, Hercules.

An armchair, whisky, and a smoke,
improve the taste of goading boys
towards a rumour of applause
that's fainter as the years go by
and banish thoughts of Iphicles,
the boy your mother loved the best,
who was her husband's only son.

No need to struggle with the tall sash now.

Outside the eighteen darkening panes
lies all the sorrow of the Masters' Garden,
where beehives and exotic trees
are spectral in the mist that hides
the empty playing-fields, and then
the valley's steeper banks, its flow.

IV

It's safer to be drunk than think.

What was that certainty, the day
he crumpled as his wife confessed
the focus of her restlessness,
then beat a slithery retreat
in hobnails and a waterproof,
that he had somehow glimpsed himself,

androgynous and beckoning,
a long way off across a planted field?

Thought salvaged him, and it was merely
a scarecrow in a cotton dress.

V

Boys barge from fart-filled rooms, and men
on tiptoe from the common-room
leave Jigger to his lonely ease
as something frets the outside dark
and taps the glass as if to enter.

O zonam perdidit!

Somewhere today he lost the key
that swung in pain-inflicting arcs
inside the long sleeve of his chalky gown.

His Latin tags are fatuous.

Ozone is what he needs, not drink,
perchance a holiday, meanwhile
his spectacles are gone, his books, his pen
that cut with scarlet *ynke*:
schoolmastering hits heads of only
the shadows of its silly boys.

VI

Brute suppressed the Albinests,
huge giants, fierce and strong,
and of this isle, un-Scotted yet,
he empire had ere long...

When Jigger nods and dreams the end
of titan Albion and all
his upstart swarthy Albinests,
he sees true Albion, the land, released,
eponymous, that Trojan Brute
and all fair-skinned, fair-minded Brutons
may tramp in peace their native hills.

Such views were rife when he attended
the University of Troy Novant.

VII

Recall that morning, spiked with pot-pourri,
when sunlight and suburban air,
asked only that he knuckle down
to make sense of that how-do-you-do
of lipstick messages, the rage
of underwear Hippolytë
took off with her and twice the man
that he was then, black-skinned and ardent,
borne up on U.S. airforce wings.

For as the Smith with hammers beats
his forgèd metal, so
he dubs his club about their pates
and fleas them in a row...

Those other mornings were more happy,
when, hopping to avoid the plop,
he swished a stick, bold *claviger*,
to shoo the big cat on the farmyard wall,
while Deianira, Iole, and Hebe,
led the herd, with flailing tails,
down towards the dangerous pasture
that held the river and the anglers' hut,

to leave him swinging on the gate, an imp
in wellingtons, not merely Henry
but one the vicar, on his jovial way,
would call his infant Hercules.

VIII

Her upper parts had humaine forme,
her nether Serpentine,
the whole was monstrous, yet her wit
more monstrous, was most fine...

A spring within the armchair twangs.

It seems the scarecrow has begun
to add to beckoning a voice
that undermines his snug, well-worn regret
that he is old and drunk already
and never was an Oxford man.

IX

Now the door is not quite shut.

A need is scratching to come in, an itch
for more than that corrosive fable
of blowing roadside oaks and elms
and gates in hedgerows that reveal
those gleaming meadows, snowy orchards,
and parks in which ancestral piles
stand, among great-hearted timber,
for all that Dornford Yates and Jigger
think Englishness amounts to in the end.

Here comes a question and a wounding
that wakes him to confront the dark.

Eheu fugaces… labuntur anni!

Outside, each fallen leaf records
the grieving of the arboretum.

X

Alas that from the lab stinks rise.

Boy-haunted passages are glooming fast:
no time to ogle photographs
of First XIs, First XVs,
or keep an eye on changing rooms.

Aut insanit homo aut versus facit!

Yes, Sir, we know that you eschewed
perverse insanitary deeds.

XI

Just like the spook in Betton Wood,
or Alfred's child, the scarecrow speaks
but has no language but a cry
that makes her grinning topknot tremble
above the snake-shreds of her frock.

He sees the flutter of her hesitation
positioned where a cloud adjusts
and readjusts, as in a loop,
the envelope of light in which
she seems unable to complete
the half-turn she has almost made.

Obscurum per obscurius!

Perhaps she calculates the cost
of entry to a human heart,
and, scenting lack of will, resolves
to try her skill at bilocation.

Her cut-throat grin becomes a gap
between the inner and the outer dark
through which thin mischief starts to seep.

XII

The black man, grinning as he mounts a wing
to reach the cockpit of his plane,
has bleached to buff before he falls
off the locker, by the bed
in which Hippolytë is doped asleep,
and shatters glass and no one sees
the cleaner bin him, fearing censure.

GOODBYE TO DR IPHICLES

A photo from the local paper
is also quickly binned, compressed
to pellet-form and lobbed by Jigger.

It shows the town's most popular GP
beside his wife and smiling colleagues,
multiracial, un-class-conscious,
for *au-revoirs* before he flies
to serve in long-postponed retirement
with Médecins Sans Frontières.

XIII

The hives are sleeping, and no honey bees
could replicate what he can hear
outside his window, in the monkeypuzzle.

It is a sibilance that scarecrows find
torments the kind of men who look
at women as into a mirror
to see the face of what they loathe.

It's not just women Jigger trusts
to make him squirm, but all their flock
of nancy-boys and fancy-men,
and jungle-monkeys on the make,
and Celtic whingers with their paws
about the throat of Albion.

To lacke life lost in chalke and ynke:
an hell, an hell, an hell…

A time has come when what he hates
is coiled so tight about his chest
that fear and rage unreconciled
grow hot enough to scorch his vest.

The lilac waits beside the oak.

More subtle than the ghosts of ghosts
are all the causes in their ancient files
of what he is, and must now lose.

XIV

Does he still hope for company?

Then fill an afternoon with summer heat,
the breathy rub of thirty boys,
the shipboard creak of desks, the creep
of Platignum and Osmiroid.

Is there a danger to the perfect grass?

Jerk up the window, out with him and under,
arms and legs a movie flicker,
to kite his black and tattered sleeves
towards the shimmering cricket square
where, in the haze, dark limbs and creamy
entwine in ecstasy unnoticed
by men who mow, and mark the creases.

How fair she was, and who she was,
she bore for him the bell
that knew although he clownish is
the place where beauty dwells…

Such moments hold the hours and years.

Wake up the organ with the Founder's Anthem,
let sunlight play on beeswaxed floors
and trophies, mustered in a silver dazzle
as if for battle, and a raft of flowers.

Have sashes squeak, and schoolboy faces
cling like sediment to sills and sides
of lofty windows, eighteen-paned,
to see a burnished car deposit,
to comic bugles of the Corps, and birdsong

never heard so clearly since,
a royal duchess, polka-dotted,
with long silk gloves whose fingers reach
down forty years to squeeze his fingers.

Non nisi malis terrori!

Beneath her condescending smile,
thin sticks are what her dress hangs on.

XV

The sooty hills have shuffled off
their weight of visibility:
allotments where the town expires
are compartmentalising dusk.

As quick as breath, let's be aboard
the train home through a fading day.

Each night, cold lights of combines turn
to shave straight edges of the crop
then turn again: hauled in their wake,
jolting balers pack the hay.

XVI

Whose so-called father's room, whose bed,
is where this broken breathing comes?

Bis pueri senes!

This lad should not be here at all
alone at this late early time,
the stillest of a summer night,

when childhood ends with harvest baled
and scattered in the stubble fields.

He should not stand too near this window
or dare to breathe such altered air.

Fear and freedom are his chums,
clasp-knife-wielding, boy-scout-belted,
with bread and jam in greaseproof paper,
to track adventure to its lair
in full sun of the holidays,
out by the pungent path next to the lilac
and the wide trunk of the climbing oak,
in which, among the highest branches,
his tattered kite is bravely flapping:
heraldic, irretrievable. Perhaps.

The bedside tick, the bedside tock,
are louder when the breathing stops.

XVII

I'll leave here when that monkeypuzzle
puts out one bloody English rose.

The worse for booze, a breathless grip
comes back as if his chest belonged
to him no longer, but a man
who dies each night, or else a son
he might have been, an Iphicles
whose decent, hopeful heart expands too far.

The best of bees do beare, beside
sweet honey, smarting stings,
and time doth not need any baite
that unto sorrow brings...

And not until the lawyer finds
a legacy for Iphicles
and none for him, and only then
is Jigger sent to make his claim
upon the doorstep of the vicarage,
before the tall door in the rain,
on one who kept his mother mum
and will bequeath him nothing but her blame.

XVIII

Silence strikes its longest note.

Time dawdles where the scarecrow flickers,
as if projected through an inner lens,
and guys him, done up like a sailor's floozy,
while Christmas holidays repeat, and summers
go by with minor maintenance:
the school asleep through tinker shuffles
late every morning of the mops and pails.

More bloody darkies every term.

What wakes the hives among the leaves
that scab the lawn like dead skin dropping?

Again the pain recedes, and whisky
dilates his throat the more to croak
his mockery of banter,
not laughable, an obstacle to laughter.

The loop snaps and the scarecrow moves.

XIX

The whole was monstrous, yet her wit,
more monstrous, was most fine,
and fed on fear and spite she thus
confounded all she found,
propounding questions, and a word
unanswered was a wounde...

Heart thuds that activate the air
like tiny eddies of departure
disturb the room and silence prompts
echoes, barely short of stillness,
which are inquisitorial.

How noiselessly the tall sash rises.

She's found your bolt-hole, Henry Jigger,
master of the sleepy arts
of armchair and tobacco jar,
by way of ramblers' paths and roads
turned serpentine, and boy-scuffed rooms,
and labs and halls and corridors,
and trees and hives where mist conceals
what slithers in the Masters' Garden.

XX

If only once, he should have skipped
behind the herd into the morning sun
that tipped their horns with gold, and turned,
as Warner sings, a crab, perhaps,
or tuned a round to test the air
as far as to the farthest pasture,
boldly heedless of comeuppance.

Dum vivimus, vivamus!

Likewise, the necessary grit
to be a comrade to a restless wife,
and fund a family and find it later,
if not quite grateful, well disposed,
might now have helped him face the dark
and dust that settles all he chose.

They sweetly surfeiting in joy
and silent for a space,
whenas the ecstacy had end
did tenderly embrace.

An hell then, speechless Vivimus?

Its topknot level with the open window,
in murk that thickens as he peers
to see what something outside is,
the araucaria extends its fingers
to shelter nothing, and to shed no leaves.

XXI

Alas, the fleeting years, alas
the nursing home that drearily
accommodates Hippolytë
and swindles Dr Iphicles.

She and her twice-the-man, now unremembered,
share their lost time with the zephyr
that makes the scarecrow beckon, and forever
disturbs the tassel on the mortarboard
of Jigger by the the royal car,
the day he hears the organ grumble
in concert with the bugles and the birds.

Hebe, Iole, and Deianira,
for the last time in that selfsame moment
re-enter the forbidden pasture.

That no-time, neither tick nor tock,
is at the window when poor Jigger
falls as if he falls for ever
from childhood into altered air.

Necessitas non habet legem!

For leglessness, a final dram
is once again what we require.

XXII

He is too pusillanimous
upon this second windowsill
to trust the voice that calls him out
to play the man and earn his wings
above the fives court and the Bursar's house,
the shut pavilion and the stud-pocked fields.

But Hercules is brave and young
among the footholds of the oak
whose branches close and then fall back
before his blows, bold *claviger*,
until his black kite lifts away
its academical and chalky tatters,
to clamber up the playful sky.

XXIII

It's Jigger's turn to spook the eye:
his bee-swarm of the heart becomes
a palanquin that bears him up
like Brutus into Albion
above the tree-tops of the Masters' Garden
triumphally, then lets him drop.

The hives vibrate.

A tattered tongue uncoils and spits
while polka-dots of dapples fall
in strange light where a shive of summer
warms the duchess in the arboretum,
her snake-shreds sloughed, and wearing daisies
entangled in her pubic hair,
for waggle-dancing, and the splits.

So who can equal Hercules
by whom the monster fell
who, burning up her ugly shape,
did passe her soule to hell?

Tonight Her Royal Highness finds
herself the lithe embodiment
of lewd and ludicrous delight, wherefrom
the voice proceeds that soothes the bees.

XXIV

Contraries be the elements,
at strife contraries fall,
yeat Sea, the Earth, the Aier, them both,
the skie be-cleaps them all...

In the café, therefore greasy, stirring
as trains pass, hangs the banner of St George
above the pallid bone-shaved heads of Brutons.

On hinterland where hills are dark and soggy
and neighbourhoods where black and white
share terraces by railway-lines,
a mosque, a synagogue, and many churches,
on market stalls of jeans and saris,
and softly on the flat-roofed day-room
in which, upon a high-seat chair,
Hippolytë is sitting, dreaming,
autumn dampness turns to drizzle.

Meanwhile, a strange unlovely rose,
blood-scumbled, will be stretchered down
and pouched among the fallen leaves.

Recreant wretch, he Albion loved
and wished her to be free,
that causèd him to suffer on
a cruel outlandish tree...

Across the lawn, three policewomen,
Iole, Deianira, Hebe,
as if in mourning, gather clothes,
a hearing-aid and shoes, a watch-chain,
in line with a trajectory
a jump for England might have barely managed
from window-sill to monkeypuzzle.

Your native rain, O Hercules, dissolves
the Hydra's venom in the blood
and cools at last your fiery vest.

XXV

Nor meete it were, in Justice or
in nature, things of nought
shall equal that unbounded Power
that All of Nothing wrought.

That be not Two or divers Gods
is also prompt by this,
and vanitie is Period
of everie thing that is.

Of One all Multiplicities,
Formes, Harmonies, (what not?)
be, howsoere they seeme confused,
producèd and begot.

Of whichsoere all creatures be
compounded formally,
so then of contrarieties
is Uniformitie.

To one Sea flow all Fluds, one Sunne
inlighteneth every Light,
of all celestiall Movings is
one Mover, artists write.

Trunke, barke, boughs, leaves, and blossomes, none
like others hath a Tree,
yet but one Roote, whence all, which but
one Author's act can bee.

XXVI

Somewhere a bell, elsewhere a morning
choir is on its feet and singing:

Behold a teacher, with the Sun
he doth his flocke engage
and all the day with ynke and chalk
he merry warre can wage,
and with the Sun doth fold again,
then jogging home betime,
he turns a crab, or tunes a round,
or sings some merry rhyme...

Warner's verse, the driest work
committed yet to pen and ynke,
floats down like cobweb scraps to settle
as dust upon an empty chair
from which a man in pain and drink
has clambered into air and gone
beyond the tall sash, eighteen-paned,
to friendly distances where hills,
no longer sooty, wake to welcome,
conjubilant, the dauntless boots
and anoraks of Albion.

XXVII

The organ heaves its direst rumble
while coughing and snot-noises die.

The choir attacks *Jerusalem*,
then struggles up a notch to raise
Warner whose immortal pen
as high as maybe, where poor Jigger,

on thermals of hyperbole
has reached the bright imaginary green
and found at last within the dazzle
his shape and size of place exactly.

XXVIII

Voices disperse, and choristers
attempt their lives without rehearsal.

Above their heads, the organist
deserts his nest and switches off
the light that lit the keys and stops.

Desks slam like shots, a muffled fart
moves on the day like any other.

XXIX

Half-mast, a fresher St George banner shifts
as mist warms in the Masters' Garden
and thins to snake-trails on the playing fields.

Whenas the ecstacy has end, the skies
within this future we are making
unclasp the ground while Albion
hugs closer what her myths disguise.

XXX

The sweet o' the year is rising up
so dewy and so odorous
from out of England's snowy orchards,

to scent the isle, all lands excelling,
where Jigger has inherited
his long dream of her heights and woods,
and freedom of her unmapped meadows.

Fuimus Troes!

Fag-ash and whisky glass survive
a dwindling moment as he slips
the minds of feckless sons of Brutus.

Their clownish shapes a coined show,
the poore schoolmasters weep,
schoolmasters weep and they are woe,
and then do silence keep.

Yet soldier on, thou frumious Trojans,
turn blackboards into cliffs of chalk
in those true-blue academies
from which no Englishman retires, wherein
no women and no scarecrows dwell,
and skirmish joyfully with silly boys
like Blake, and Shakespeare, and Purcell.

The Silver of the Mirror

> In time his expences brought clamours about him, that overpowered
> the lamb's bleat and the linnet's song; and the groves were haunted
> by beings very different from fawns and fairies.
>
> SAMUEL JOHNSON, *Lives of the English Poets*, 'Shenstone'

As if reflected by the street, the soil
he stands on, with his long nose raised
to sniff the nearness of the revolution,
accepts the clean blade of his hoe
and scatters slowly, as through antique glass.
It is a matter of above, below.
He wears knee-breeches and a tricorn hat,
and mumbles verse into his plain jabot
of which he is the pleased but modest author.
His mild voice coaxes lawns and trees
to ripple through translucent tarmac,
still carrying the sentiments
he adds to them, on painted plaques,
of Thoughtfulness, of Sadness, and of Pity.
We tear the pavements up to reach his garden
and roar like beasts in pain, as boundaries break,
to find ourselves reduced by what we spoil.

And yet we are his comrades, and our horror
an upside-down ideal while, hoof to toe,
we struggle to assist him as we churn
parterres to mud and trample flat
the topiary and pergolas
he has maintained are beautiful, and wreck
the patterned walks, the symmetries
he laid out to reflect unchanging order.
The dream is his, and ours the revelation
that animates all malcontents.
The rumpus of our anguish fills the city.

Meanwhile, within the silver of the mirror,
beyond the ruined portico
and fountains with their splendours mired to wallow,
the cornfields and the hills where flocks are grazed
are as his verses promise, yet more golden,
and at his feet the seeds of terror grow.

The Squirrel

Not yet, perhaps not here, but in the end,
And somewhere like this.

PHILIP LARKIN

You talk to sunshine on the photograph
that blears our unremembered faces
and mirrors yours, within a thin black frame.
Your flowers are very cheerful in their vases.
We did not wish you to be put in here,
or see your footprints, as you drag your shins
beneath a floral dressing-gown
across the mop-slicks in the corridor.

Here's where you dream you tripped a snare
that closed forever on a whiff
of disinfectant, and a pain that lingers.
You're like the squirrel on the chandelier,
we try to reach you, but our fingers
grasp only air, and up you go,
beyond our help, to where your name
comes vacantly from far below.

You planned to age like poetry:
lyric and elegy becoming one
in celebration of the verb *to be*.
To kiss you, we blot out the sun.
We did not wish you to be made of stuff
morphine can manage till your smile begins
to claim that dying is the same
as painless waking, and no damage done.

99

The Redesdale Rowan

From now on I will be dispensing
with ramblers' maps, and all desire
to find the flora of this rabbit-lawn
listed in my guidebook to the fells,
or read the secret of the storm-shot rowan –
that should have fallen, yet has berries dancing
blood-red on leafy carousels –
in some botanical grimoire.
The day is warm. My feet are aching.
It is too late, with sunshine in my eyes,
to care which insect air force is commencing
a mass-attack of lullabies.
I shall approach the tree and dream there, waking
to hang my branches with a peal of bells.

The Tourist

The tourist at this moment will not stir
but stares beyond the cypresses
towards unmelted snow on sharp sierras
as if his eyes were new again.
A girl is sweeping, hushing an old broom,
and speaks politely but he will not answer.
He finds the scents of myrtle and of jasmine
insufficient, like the dark pinetum
and all the thread-like veins of lichen.
Tell him the colour of the crumbling tower
is not valerian, yet not quite rose.
He has remembered a young dancer.
Above the lizard on the broken column
he sees the trembling of the stars.

Après-midi

On the jetty is a grey collection
of packing-cases, a piano,
a limp flag hanging from a crooked staff,
the navigation office, closed.
This is a good day for the turtle,
the sand-caked boy who finds a starfish,
the tethered cockerel, beneath a tree
fantastical in swags of moss.
Upstream, mud-banks are volatile
and teem with crocodiles. The river's low.
Our progress will not thereby be affected.
Inside the Residence, a dusty echo
returns the laughter of a large pink lady
who wants to take her clothes off and be fiction.

St George's Day

For centuries the same sun has been sinking
here, where we loiter to invoke
the green, embroidered by long-fingered shadows
of branches coming into leaf, the drumming
and piping over, and the people –
who danced today and work the land in common –
cupping hands into the cool mill-brook,
which are our own hands, but with calluses.
Beside the inn door, at a solid table,
a ballad-seller, and two dairy-women,
sing the language we are thinking.
As Hob the landlord gobs for luck
into their ale, and picks his nose,
new worlds grow outward from the sunlit oak.

Black Country Browning

Here's where the forges were, the crucible
where we fought fire and smoke and sin
to cast a fancy from a flower-bell,
or catch a sunset-touch in glass
for chapel windows that began to glow
as far as the antipodes.
We coupled on the warm stone by the furnace,
which brings us down to thee, grown up so well
without our piety or taste in verse.
We burnished hammers with our skin,
but it consoles us that our bishops knew
of chorus-endings from Euripides,
as we sink deeper where the anvils rust
into the centre of the compass-rose.

FOLLY WOOD

All haile the noble Companie,
Students in holy Alchimie,
Whose noble practice doth them teach
To vaile it with a mistie speech.

The Hunting of the Greene Lyon

Fermentation

The night is creeping up behind the day
and all our keys are searching for their locks.
To be misled about the greater good,
and botch the things we're meant to do,
is blameless as the rot between your teeth.
The whisky on your breath would fell an ox.
Come back with me across the muddy fields
to drink another at the *ferme ornée*
and watch the moon rise at my study window,
bewitchingly from Folly Wood.
I'll teach you how to hold it at the zenith
between your thumbs, until it yields
to gentle pressure and stops all the clocks.

Sublimation

Leave us this morning if you wish, but first
spare time to meet our floating harp.
Please make sure that the door is shut,
then call her gently and observe
how groans of vanished poets lift her up,
and birdsong from long-silent beaks
resounds to make her tilt and quiver.
On rainy days, when Malkin is morose,
the harp will sometimes stamp her foot
upon the parquet, and make starlings burst
like soot bombs from the hearth and box
his ears with black arpeggios.

Congelation

To find our whereabouts, look at the palm
of your left hand – the *thenar eminence*,
since we are scientific men – yes, yes,
or Mount of Venus if you wish, and see
an old stone farmhouse with embellishments –
a turret and a little park,
my study window with four branching lancets –
all taking shape beneath the sun
while you and I consult your fate together.
Be patient as the landscape gathers
about you in its own good time and weather.
The temple on the *hypothenar* knoll –
towards the South – my own Mount Cyllene –
pertains to Mercury, Hermes, or Thoth
in all his guises. To the North,
young Goldilocks, the green of thumb,
is Ceres, in the kitchen garden
levelled from the hill behind the house.
See how she skittishly unseats
potatoes for our casserole,
and throws aside her garments as she goes.
The roof, too, is of slabs of stone
between which blown seeds find an anchorage
as you have done, now look again
and pick us out among the terms and statues
that make this terrace quite a pantheon.
You will see further, when you find the courage.
A gleam of water, linking head and heart,
bisects your *palmar excavation* –
we are still scientific men –
through working meadows where a path ascends
along the Line of Destiny
to Folly Wood, the hanging dark
that cloaks the hillside at your fingers' ends.

Exaltation

When I'm despondent, Malkin makes me laugh
by reading with that squawk of his
adjusted to a boyish chime
and funnelled lips, as if to blow
or suck the letters off the page and leave
upon his lap not book but album.
Perhaps his face-parts are becoming stiff.
Tonight, if there are stars they will be fierce
and coat my Gothick bridge with rime,
the path as well, up which he'll go –
cold clockwork hungry for the taste of life –
if I provoke him and then set him off.

Conjunction

She is my keenest sharpener of knives,
and skilful with the apparatus
that traps the essence of the strong night air
which is assisting my rejuvenation.
A man is noble when he strives
to garner wisdom and to master nature
and true philosophers should not take wives.
Of course, propinquity and pulchritude
will not be overlooked, and thus
Miss Goldilocks has learned to please and tease.
When my indulgence prompts ingratitude,
she takes to girlish fits of rustication
and then my fond heart leaps to see her gain
the lawn and fields beyond the pantheon –
those absurd deities of my domain
extending limbs of mossy stone
as if to halt her by gesticulation –
then ford the trout stream on her hands and knees,

as naked as a naiad in the flood,
and climb an oak before my pack arrives
to tree her there till I am understood.

Cibation

This evening we shall make your finger bleed
to tempt those pretty singers from their nests,
that thrive on blood up by the temple,
and only blood, except a little pepper
which I provide to make them sing more purely.
You will enjoy their soothing anapæsts
the more so should our harp, as if she dreamt
their singing, let the darkling breeze
move among her strings and make them tremble
sufficiently to harmonise.
Be careful when they start to feed.
You'll see them take a very dove-like supper
unless the pepper makes them sneeze,
in which case they may change their ways entirely
and every eager beak become a blade.

Separation

The past is something a wise man discards,
but there are episodes to mention.
Since I grew up apart from other boys,
the victims of my first success with words
were lovers on a Davenport tureen.
They lived in gardens quite like mine
but less austere, you understand,
with ruined arches and tall banks of flowers
that leaned towards them on the porcelain
as he inclined, with half-closed eyes,

to doff his hat and kiss her hand
while she would tilt her fan in condescension.
I shrank myself so I could creep unseen
through roses, or behind an urn,
and ridicule the passing of their hours
beneath the glaze, until the joys
they longed for broke, in pale blue shards,
and scattered on the steps down to the lawn.

Multiplication

Correspondences reveal to natures
having the wit to read them, or the luck,
that highest knowledge is armillary
in its unfolding, known and knower
revolving, loop through loop and arc through arc,
about the limbs of God. Oh dear,
that clatter from the scullery –
my hip-bath knocked down from its hook –
means you-know-who is off again
on one more of her mad adventures. Look
how late blue twilight turns the stone
of pavement, balustrade, and pantheon,
to pewter, like your whisky flask,
which as you lift it shows the moon
her dull reflection. Pass it over.
That's better. Now let's stroll the lawn
between the trees – those mute philosophers,
who are like us both seed and sower –
and see how my ancillary
makes zigzag progress through the park,
a skinny flicker in the dusk
pursued by coiling, tumbling creatures
that breathe in daylight and exhale the dark
and are her mind's corollary.

Projection

Please open my four lancet windows wide
and sit beside me, in the musky air,
facing inward to my room and books
between the pale sky and the bare
three-cornered table, by the shadow-flecked
cheval-glass with carved vine leaves on its frame
and birds that, in the firelight, twitch their wings.
Drink up. It's not formaldehyde.
Tomorrow, you and I shall recommence
our studies and have done with logic chopping
or theory without effect,
and seek for knowledge fertile in performance.
Ignore poor Malkin, and the hiccuping
he makes to mock us as we charge our glasses
and all those disapproving looks
from she who tends the hearth for us, unswathed.
Such nothings in the shape of things
are unimportant, though they have their uses.
The night I fetched you here and had you bathed
and put up with your petulance,
you'd more than had your share of whisky supping.
Well done. Chin Chin. I'm glad you came
and took hold of the moon with such assurance.
Things are since then, I trust, a little clearer.
The man you thought you were must be rebuked
in solemn sentences then stand aside
while what you are becoming is invoked
and enters – as your old life passes
before us in the bleary mirror –
as scorching brightness, and each gilt bird sings.

Solution

This morning light lacks strength. No doubt
the copper magus with his staff and cape
upon the weather-vane has turned about
to indicate an unpropitious quarter.
Close watching through the doleful hours
will inculcate contempt for rest
and strengthen your elastic powers.
Our privilege is work, advancing
philosophy towards the dark
of which the edge of brightness is a trap
we shall avoid, now we can trace
the root of tinctures to a dormant spark.
Do not be eager for success. Today,
we may not hope to boil the fire in water.
Try once again to give your thoughts a shape.
Twelve circling cherubim with lettered wings
about their shoulders, might we say,
and Arts and Sciences to sing and clap?
When Goldilocks brings porridge in at last
greet her politely, I suggest,
but turn your eyes from her beguiling body
and let your thoughts continue dancing
the Great Word with their feathered arms unfurled.
The daft girl has a pretty face,
but such allurements, and the scran she brings,
are merely echoes of a world
through which we have already passed.

Calcination

I watched you through binoculars
pick small stones in a daze and grip them hard –
as if in obscure shame for ease
or guilty pleasure in your circumstances –
then toss them into incense smoke
for Hermes, at his temple on the rise.
Well, since such mischief has been done,
we must be bold philosophers
and learn composure from the wise
not lose our heads like womenfolk.
If you were faithful to the ordinances –
correct but not meticulous –
the ritual may yet evoke
an Entity disposed to hurt you less
than these same pebbles, if I squeeze
your hand. Like that! Be on your guard.
Rules have been broken by today's endeavours.
Those stones are shifty as your eyes upon
the table, as I rearrange their glances.

Putrefaction

Tell me again about that twilit pause
in which the trees – if trees they were –
with all the thickets of the world implicit,
closed ranks about you, with each trembling twig
alert for answers from the air
that blanched your breath, and numbed your fingers
against the pewter of the whisky flask
and darkened as you took a swig.
Then how abruptly the engulfing road –
as you expanded on your choice
to quit the treadmill for the whirligig –
detached itself from destination,
an attribute of which no trace now lingers.
In that I was myself of course complicit
through true philanthropy, which knows no vice.
Meanwhile, remember why the toad
devours the eagle and the lion –
all but their crowns of leaf-green fire –
then sleeps until his loathsome sores
are jewels on a perfect skin.
I must enable this. Your task
will be to praise him when he wakes,
as we shall, into paradise.
Unlatch your tongue and then rejoice.
They are in each of us, the thin
dissecting cry a baby makes,
the soothing remnant of a deeper voice.

Recapitulation

Today we walk through fire, not air,
and you shall weave a wife or daughter
to leave behind in Folly Wood
as soon as we have done with reaping,
and all our work will be a dream
that once trod on your face, and stumbles
away into a nodding head
of gleanings bound with baler twine.
The space between us is becoming flame
as clouds that harden into lead
intensify the afterglow.
This lough has not been fed by any stream
but by the dripping conifers
where we shall hang your dolly knot –
a noddle like a harp, that trembles
to wind and birdsong – gently tapping
the cross-branch of a pine. You know her name
because you loved her long ago
and would forget her, if you could.
The meadows are incarnadine
about the *ferme ornée*, no trespassers
disturb a prospect that resembles
a palm unclenched – a window shut
on purpose to continue peeping –
as light like gold moves off the cooling water.
The dusk is warm, the stars benign,
and you have nothing to return to there
where what you were is in my keeping.

The Brass Band

Oh that I had given up the ghost, and no eye had seen me!
Job 10: 18

You claimed this view could soothe you with its sermon
of wildness tamed
and turned to English parkland, nearer heaven
than you were, choking with the cough, ashamed
because Jerusalem remained unbuilt
in spite of all you'd done. The nursery clock
would hiccup by your bed again so merrily!
I'd dream you rode a rocking horse full tilt
home down the years, your white unbloodied smock
embroidered freshly in my memory.

You'd find such eloquence to speak of vice
and poverty.
I'd have your sisters read your letters twice
and total up the times, as we took tea,
you'd mention rickets, say, or sewage farms
and then we'd smile together as we'd try
to picture your excursions, primed with prayer,
your tracts and Bibles dragging down your arms,
about those labyrinths where industry
disorders nature and befouls the air.

Be still. Although I hardly see at all,
it hurts my eyes
each time you fidget with the parasol.
The sun to me is that with which you'd rise
each day with ardour for the public good,
a disc obscured by smoke, deprived of rays
by all the furnaces of busy hell.
Sit back and gaze towards the hanging wood
above the temple by the lake, the maze
you used to say you'd solve when you were well.

It's said by men who have the landscape eye
that concave ground
will ever be the source of tranquil beauty,
which same configuration draws forth sound.
Go now, as flower beds invade the lawns
and brass glints from a birdcage made of iron.
The new age has produced, in its confusion,
a kind of orchestra of artisans
who own their instruments and wives in common.
Their music is the fruit of your compassion.

The Acorn

I love him, but I cannot like him; and as for taking his arm,
I should as soon think of taking the arm of a tree.

A friend writing about Henry Thoreau

Chainsaws have been slicing trees in half
all day where paths are soft and there are falls
of loose earth from the unsafe banks.

Their yelps disturb the potted fern
beside his window, as autumnal air
becomes more pungent and the breeze

resounds like bad news in the wire
but does not wake the telephone.
The world has put up with his harmlessness

among these pictures, books, and cases
of *objets trouvés* from his lonely strolls
for long enough, and that malaise

that keeps him self-sufficient and well-meaning.
The lambs are restless on the hill, a calf
takes fright in its familiar haining

as gravity weighs down his walls
as if to bed the man in stone. Death wears
a smile cut into bark and knows

how weakly sap flows up his shanks,
and also in which chest of drawers
upstairs, beneath his socks, an acorn grows.

The Green Corn

Now we're done and harvested, remember us
grinding the bugbear of the bourgeoisie –
repulsive, squirming, and ridiculous –
beneath our marching boots. The century
caught fire and edged our shadows with a nimbus
that spooked the pale ghost of uncertainty
as new dawns broke, and kerchiefed girls went swinging
their strong limbs to the rhythm of our singing.

We learned in cinemas to love the murder
of cartoon characters, and came to find
that squeamishness is soluble in laughter.
Our revolution was a sleep of mind,
to build the dream that reasserts the order
which progress must impose on humankind.
But soon the dream in turn informed the will
and we found breathing enemies to kill.

How pinkly then our shirts and dirndls shone
as earth soaked up the colours of our banner,
and children carried grief and shattered bone –
the Jew's nose, top hat, and the big cigar –
to tinkling music from a gramophone
in gratitude as trophies to our leader –
moustached and dapper in his dungarees –
while we like green corn rippled round his knees.

The Bather

We must be careful with this memory:
the context is already shaking loose
in which we all drift back as if we're sorry.

A younger dog behind the house
rehearses a remembered bark
of ownership to welcome us

together with a fresh gust from the loch
that shifts your papers in the escritoire
and worries leaves along the chestnut walk.

The keyhole of the rosewood drawer
admits light to a corner of the letter
you wrote to tell the world you didn't care.

That gillie in his shirt-sleeves knew no better
than tug his forelock by the path you took
thirty years ago, down to the water.

Let's hang your legend on its hook
beside our coats in your cold kitchen
and drink your whisky in the ingle-nook.

You weren't a bad girl, on reflection,
and there are worse ways to pretend to die
than leave your night-dress to attract attention,

your towel on a tree to dry,
and live the life of Riley, then goodbye.

Unity in the Englischer Garten

She went to Parteitagen as to Mass
and still prays to the Führer, but in vain.
She let the dear storms commandeer a flat
on Agnesstrasse. When the Jews who own
nothing now but old age and their bags had gone
she turned her future in the lock.
She dreams that lava-heaps and cinder-cones
rise from hot sand when she tries to run
and then veiled women in a great black car
as dawn comes crush her in a Swinbrook lane.
Now rooks with silver swastikas convene
mock parliaments among the trees
beside the Haus der Kunst. The day is warm
and she is beautiful. She sees
across the park the Isar fuss
among its channels in an English manner
with swarming khaki backwaters. Her brain
must calculate her worth. The world's at war.
The British consulate is off the phone.
There's no one left to play with or to shock.
A green bench shimmers in the sun.
Wearing her crimped hair like a hat
she sits there to relax and points the gun
against her blank cherubic face.
She is a kind of saint. We need not care
nor spare the time to think of her again.

Penny Dreadful

A blade along the dull hide of a strop
sounds like my breath. I've strength to crawl
up past the sleeping bells and drop
down heavily where dew sobs on the leads,
an English town below me like a map,
Victorian and safe. Folk in their beds
dream me above them and my arms are long.
My hands have grown less human and are red
enough to choke the dawn. It's time to stop
and hug the weathercock. I shall not fall
into the net of right and wrong
or bait my conscience like a trap.
This is the end of what is done and said.
I left her bedroom like a butcher's shop.

BOBBY BENDICK'S RIDE

When thou shalt come into the marriage chamber, thou shalt take the ashes of perfume, and lay upon them some of the heart and liver of the fish, and shalt make a smoke with it. And the devil shall smell it and flee away.

Tobit 6: 16-17

Shoes grip cobbles to a car-horn tucket.
Nine crocodiles, *monsieur le prêtre,*
are ancient monuments of France. Hearts trip
along a rank of drums. The precious luggage,
Christ, His Mother, and a silk-lined turtle shell,
is shouldered, staggering in air
against the weight of which a fan
stirs damp aromas of the *plat du jour*
traditionnel, peculiar
to this vicinity. Marmot perhaps.
Blood pudding possibly. Identity
is not presumed upon. Our rendezvous
shall be the foyer of La Belle Hôtesse.

> *A muckle beast wi' fowre guid legs*
> *is Bobby Bendick's mare,*
> *but Auld Nip loups on twa cleft hooves*
> *an' follows Bobby far.*

Sometimes in reading and in walking I arrive
as of a sudden at a place in part
familiar and yet not clearly known
and hear my footsteps die away
ahead of me. Uncommon heat
is tightening the strings of summer's
theorbo. The swift-winged choirs
are over Otterburn that are not birds
nor are they cherubim. They see us plod
or jig like pismires on the molehill earth
that trammels us. I now perceive
that by remaining fools we may prevail.
A thin voice stretches and is broken.

> *A muckle beast wi' twa guid lugs*
> *is Bobby Bendick's mare,*
> *but Nip whae wears baeth lugs an' horns*
> *heors Bobby from afar.*

What stirs the air? I know this floor
on which my shadow moves. The huntsman's leg
bends through a crutch below the knee.
He is composed of tesserae
no one has seen who knows his name
for seven hundred years. He draws his bow
and eyes the buck. Who is the last
one to forget? The fish. Fine pleasances
are hereabouts I studied in
of sweet grass in the shade bestowed by oaks
and chestnuts. *L'enfant Enric* himself was not
more comfortable in his *carapace*
than I in those days with my head in books.

> *A muckle beast wi' twa guid een*
> *is Bobby Bendick's mare,*
> *but Nip wi' een like spairkin' lamps*
> *spies Bobby from afar.*

I am a gentleman the Lord has made
uncommon apt to read and walk at once
provided only that my pace
be easy and be regular. Vile Azariah
is no man but a crocodile
in his duplicity. My Bible goes
with me most often and has gathered grass
between its leaves, and such a harvest
of hedgerow foliage withal
to mark those passages I have discovered
most like to veins of profitable ore
that it has now a rustick look
in colour earthen, a most precious clod.

> *A muckle tail to thresh the air*
> *has Bobby Bendick's mare,*
> *but Auld Nip's tail's a muckle flail*
> *tae thresh puir Bobby sore.*

What man would not delight, placed in a garden
to make a survey of its rich collections?
Would groves and grottoes and the artful
wilds of it, the patterned flowers
and open vistas not delight his soul?
How tempting it is then to envy
the all-contriving Genius and strive
by stealth to steal away His secret treasure.
But might the man yet find himself
drawn back towards the gate he entered by
to find that now there is no gate
and where he came by is a darker path?
The reader casts a shadow on the page.

> *A foal o' fair Northumberland*
> *is Bobby Bendick's mare,*
> *but Bobby gans awa' tae France*
> *an' skules wi' Ezra theor.*

Gargoyles like crocodiles weep kisses
upon Sophia's upturned face –
where she is letting down her hair and sings
her secret names while clambering
the nine rungs of the shadow of a ladder –
and kisses on the cheeks of cobblestones.
I see her lean unsteadily
towards the dish of strawberries
I set out on my window-sill.
The Lisles Burn is descending in its linns
to fishponds and a dovecote. Now her song
is silenced by the roaring flutter
that dusts me in my stride and passes over.

> *True-hairted an' a Christian steed*
> *is Bobby Bendick's mare,*
> *she'll kick hor stable door tae spelks*
> *if Ezra passes neor.*

Acquaint me with her words. Her strawberry lips.
A brazier glows. Today the path
where white dust alternates with tender spots
of coolness in which shadows linger
has led to Woodburn or Lescar
and some small industry about an engine
compact of beams and ropes upon a husting
that has a purpose I shall ascertain
by asking. I am a priest and shall be told.
The fish that bit away the foot
shall not be captured but another
filleted for gall and heart and liver
according to the scheme of Azariah.

> *A loyal an' a jealous steed*
> *is Bobby Bendick's mare,*
> *if wicked Ezra tries tae moont*
> *betimes he's kicked awa'.*

I'll hire a car and drive to Paradise
through lynchet-meadows. In a pool
while bathing an offensive-looking trout
will no doubt speak to me. I shall be kind.
Responding pleasantly I will suggest
that we are friends and I breathe water
as he does. *Charmant mais sans merci, c'est moi.*
Nine days I shall abide there to perfect
my holiday. I like the music
the torrent makes, the dewy grass,
the early mass of birds, the clouds
snared on the summits in a net of gold.
Monsieur, I spit upon the *plage*.

> *Beneath a bonny rowan tree*
> *stands Bobby Bendick's mare,*
> *but Ezra's i' the Ingram Pool*
> *whilst Bobby droons him theor.*

Sophia has unclothed herself in smoke
of fish guts and incense. La Belle Hôtesse
is shut down and demolished among ghosts
fading from Pau Hunt photographs, plus-fours
and golf-clubs by the bust of Bernadotte.
The left hand of a Cagot pressed to death
upon a husting *lentement*
pour bien décourager les sorcières
is got by Azariah in exchange
for English money. Great wings will beat me down.
My gown and bands, the cloth I wear
protect me. O Beelzebub
make haste to help me. Make me rich.

> *Ezra's stairk across the back*
> *o' Bobby Bendick's mare.*
> *He'll tak the road tae Blaxter Bog*
> *an' dee nae mischief mair.*

Perceive the world through its disguises.
A ruined church. A ruined priest
to celebrate the Mass for bats. Behold.
This is my parish and my duty.
Look about you, Azariah,
and see a swarm of helicopters drown
in blue air over Corsenside. Today
the wise and merciful Theanthropos
will lead us to the bank of Ingram Pool
and set before us stepping-stones
from which to plunge our crafty souls
again to bathe yet not be cleansed.
I see a blackness and a quivering cloud.

> *By Chairford Bridge an' Grindstone Sike*
> *gans Bobby Bendick's mare,*
> *for Bobby's boond for Wanney Byre*
> *tae hide hissel' awa'.*

Upon a rocking stepping-stone the urge
to stride becomes less marked, yet stride I must.
The golden days go by. The taxi
sinks on its springs. The finest shoe
I ever boned and polished is enshrined
in a broken jar of cassoulet.
What's all this luggage, Azariah,
the nine great crocodiles of France
migrating to the River Rede?
Their hellish jaws. Sometimes a slant of music,
perhaps the Small Pipes, or a known aroma,
or light upon the peaks accuses me.
I am a man whom Wisdom shall reward.

> *By Stiddlehill an' Hepple Heugh*
> *gans Bobby Bendick's mare,*
> *whilst Bobby's grippin' roond hor neck*
> *an' greets wi' mairtal feor.*

The sun each day when it declines
engraves such pictures with a fiery needle
my mind makes on the sweltering clouds
of owl-eyed lust and Azariah
the great fish in a black coat threshing water.
Each night I beat his head again with stones.
He drowned. Yet he returns. The room is empty.
Hark. She sounds. There's nothing there. I am content.
When Wisdom shall again climb through my window
she will converse with me alone.
Monsieur, there's time to take myself to France
and dig a deeper grave. The hand
that rests beside mine on the altar points.

> *A beast wi' teeth like kirkyaird stanes*
> *is Bobby Bendick's mare,*
> *but Auld Nip's like a crocodile*
> *wi' Bobby in his maw.*

Matins at nightfall. Evensong at dawn.
The roof of Cuddy's kirk is gone. Walls totter.
I'll burrow like a marmot at Wanney Byre
before the quick-nosed fiends, the dogs of hell
shall have my blood for pudding. Snares
there are in my resolve, snares in my doubt.
Horizons burn. Hark. The infernal Nimrod
sniffs me out. If God preserve me, let him roar!
Great wings beat down. Virtue decays. The earth
sings psalms to darkness in that quivering cloud
of endless pain and frantic mirth.
No one meddles here but me. The Cagot's hand
points true. My horse is swift. What stirs the air?

> *Nip i' the cleft ca'd Wanney Byre*
> *spares Bobby Bendick's mare,*
> *but hales puir Bobby deun tae hell*
> *wi' Ezra ivor mair.*

Epithalamium

His beard is safe from razor blades. His mind
is firm among the cypresses.

She is the haughtiest of pretty Misses.
The smell of their constraint is like an ache

our darting tongues explore. They must unwind
and lie down in the sun beside us

to share our mattress of embroidered moss
and learn to tolerate our lipless kisses,

our gifts of leaves and twigs, the cake
we'll make for them of mud, our cold caresses.

Sentinels

Far sooner than I had supposed
the breathing ocean has begun to creep
about the sharp prehensile toes

of phosphorescent salamanders,
immense and beautiful, who keep
close watch outside the cave where couched on wrack –

like all good parents back to back –
lie those who laughed with me at my own blunders
when time permitted and now sleep.

The Owl Herb

She who no night bird ever taught
To sing, not what it must, but ought.
                                    WALTER DE LA MARE

I'm in a deep hedge like a child out late
beside the lane. I cup my leaves
around the flower of my beak. My voice insists
through curtained windows, bolted doors,

and soon obedient somnambulists
up from their beds on clicking claws –
the whiskery, the fanged and furred –
pull on their uniforms of human skin

dropped carelessly on bedroom floors
and search for me. Such dreamy lives
produce good meat I hang in skeins
old spiders would call gossamer

to eat at leisure among frosted thistles –
less like a plant, more like a bird
from whom there won't be long to wait
before the true shout of the owl is heard.

Augenlicht

The place we've come to leans against the sky
and dreams the moon. A midden steams.
We start a hare. We are alive.

The roads we took were intricate
and bad. Though fearful we were not deterred.
A pale girl gathers shadows from the track.

She whispers an irrevocable word
of which no meaning will survive.
She is inured to working late.

The night is old. Her one bright eye
fades from our way. She's what she seems.
She moves the oceans when she turns her back.

Mademoiselle de Silhouette

As she stepped outside she heard the furniture
begin to move. She left the door ajar
in case it wished to follow her
to this small café open to the air
where there might just be room beneath the awning
behind the fence of privet bushes
for chair and table and her knick-knack shelf,
her looking-glass and scissor drawer.
The *trottoir* dapples in the sun.
A tree is pinkly pearl in bloom and thrushes
dart and chirrup their intention
to keep on simulating fun. *Voilà*.
For one bright day her darkest self
has snipped away its context. She is yawning.

The Mistress

She smiles with mild approval at the world
of which she is the hub. Her shrubberies
and pampas clumps in cared-for air
conceal our loyal faces. It's the hour
when voices carry but there is no word.
She feels no duty to acknowledge us
but remains in the mind's eye motionless
and never changing. Part of a veranda
behind her is in focus and a gable
tipped by a spike yet she is blurred.
The day is overcast. The camera
snaps up the glare of her pale dress.
We're snobs and therefore seldom envious.
The treasure box in which her future curled
at birth is ours though we've become unable
to bring ourselves to think of that. Alas
whereas we hardly recognise each other
she understands exactly who she is.

The Place I Am

I have become a master of the craft
of moulding, patiently and with precision,
lethargy into shapes of hours and days.
My cast of mind requires a library
of books I wrote myself, sufficient booze
and shabby furniture. Beyond
the balcony is marshy coast. My gaze
slides along pewter-coloured horizontals
that evening sunlight turns to bronze.
It is a habitat where rare plants learn
to live with salt, and birds nest on the ground.
It is the place I am. It should be empty
of any presence otherwise.
Rage and tales of unmapped quicksand
are not discouraging enough.
The landscape fades. I fade. I mourn its beauty
leached into sketch and photograph
or into notebooks that birdwatchers carry.
The sea is close. I fear death by erosion.
It has grown dark but now the sky is starry.
I'll jot down where I'd like my body found
but not by whom. I think that's better left.
And better left, I also think, is when.
The airport glows inland. A homing plane
blinks across the ankles of Orion.

The Riddle

The first anthropological axiom of the Evil One is not
All men are evil, but All men are the same.

W.H. AUDEN

Promise, Son, when you address appearances,
that you won't fall for similarity
and finish up like I am, unaware
of variation. Steer clear of revery
in case you subsequently fail to wake
to what things actually are or were.
Differentiation is essential work
requiring recognition accurate
as a marksman's rifle. Seek clarity.
If any object does not have a name
then name it. Learn by heart all essences.
Go nowhere on the train. Avoid the state
that I got into, me and my poor father,
not spotting on the platform among people
very much unlike each other
the beast that leapt – the stench of it – beside us –
straight through the carriage window glass remember –
its wet tongue pressed to the first syllable
of the riddle which makes everything the same.
That finished Dad. And as for me?
I dream all day of what I most resemble.

Auberge

I hope you like your room. You overlook
the entrance to the crematorium.
Even if you oversleep you're sure to wake
in time to catch at least one funeral.
The lingering scent of wreaths in drizzle
will be consoling, like the glare and hum
in your ensuite at midnight and the thump
of water pressure maximum. The climate
is hopeful hereabouts. We cope with that
by clinging to despair. We're private people.
If you require assistance, pray. Don't come
to find us or your fellow guests. To peek
and pry is bad taste and a theft of knowledge.
We keep no record of the time or date.
When you decide to go please sign the book.
You'll find the tablets in your bedside fridge.

The Unsafe Landing

Late sunbeams are prodigious epicures
in the realms of mould and small collapses –
frequent in their favourite places –
and connoisseurs of arabesques
rats sketch in dust. Let's watch them blaze
through bleary glass and lap the floors
and walls then climb as sun goes down to graze
the ceiling of some unsafe landing. Risks
must be run for such apocalypses.
Their tongues explore the flavour of our faces.

The Comfort Service

Our broadcasts are addressed to those bereaved
who cannot acquiesce to separation.
We keep things cheerful and include
favourites of the deceased. There's Little Nell,
Tagore and Keats, that episode
with Greta Garbo and the lion.
The actors we employ do not intone
inside their bowler hats like once-revered
announcers on the wireless talking rain.
But should you wish you may select Received
Pronunciation. Or indeed Morse Code.
We simply bring to bear the miracle
of narrative. There's no wrong time or place
to switch on and tune in. Clear as a bell.
The topic for today? 'What I Most Feared
Before I Made a Friend of Fright.'
We do provide advice, now and again,
which might be, sometimes, for example:
'Dear listener, look past the much-loved face
to greater love, where death cannot profane
its memory, or hog the light.'

The Laboratory

I've waited here all night lit by the glum
red bulbs above the warning notices.
Pull up the blinds and throw light on the tools
that I thought up and helped you make
when you were still unsure about the rules
and over-sensitive and prone to worries.
I'm near you in the dust above the benches
and angular uncomfortable stools
but you don't see. You're half asleep
and at the window as some water bird
hops across grass and then takes wing
to launch itself upon the lake
and on the surface of your mind like beauty.
You rub your chin until your jaw unclenches
then press your forehead and begin to weep.
I know your conscience has been saying Wrong
and reason has said Stop but, trust me, duty
though painful does not make us ghouls.
Throw back the doors. The beneficiaries
of our research already come
limping down the un-signposted access road
or clinging to the sides of dark slow lorries.

A Helpmeet for Protestant Mystics

She limps. She is inadequately shod
and not dressed for the weather of the mind.
She needs to feel her way with arms extended
to grope the insides of our skulls.
As soon as she is with or even near us
we start to see. Without her we are blind.

She quiets us to let us hear
applause again that led to curtain calls,
when we were young, for Agape and Eros
in theatres of bliss. She has amended
the chart of routes between our names for God.
She is the kinder sister of Dame Kind.

The Better Place

Adam's dream will do here...

JOHN KEATS

Your day ain't over but old age has made
the twilight worrying. Towards the posh
end of the village are *cottages ornés*,
broad-eaved, with mullions, and chimneys
diagonally set. You'll find them fussy.
Too arty-farty for eternity.
Reflections have begun to fade from rosy
where the river now flows pearly neutral.
There's no bookshop. Though you'd have wished one once
you will not read. We'll speak in rhyme.
Thoughts are visible, resembling circling moths.
Another reason why this nook is suitable
is that although it's hilly Derbyshire
we're in a bowl and therefore there's a climb
to reach a view of genuine horizons
which you of course will have no need to see.
That house has character. The former smithy.
You might well settle there as aeons pass.
Meanwhile the radiant pub. The landlady
that Adam dreamed to serve your English breakfasts
and pull the empyreal ale that causes
such ardent listlessness. Fine suddenness.
And I shall be beside you by the fire
when in the evenings you think back to us.

(for S.J.K. and T.A.G.L.)

Gantries

(i.m. Evangeline Paterson)

You believed in real heaven, no outrageous
life of spirit, endlessly delighting:
one poet fewer, one more butterfly
in some dim forest where a tiger smoulders.

We keep on borrowing each other's light,
and looking taller on each other's shoulders,
but you did neither and called out for less
confusion of the substance with the glitter.

You taught your poems to be homely,
as if their duty was to reassure,
and yet they scratch a question on the page
that angels from their gantries bend to answer.

The Magic Castle

Close the door. All she has managed to achieve
seems empty to her now. Throw in the towel.
Success is make-believe that fairytales
can easily transcend. So tell her one.
She's reached the ocean of self-doubt, its seas
acidic and tumultuous
and where their churning waters join
futures are born to serpents of the hour
enthroning bright new deities
whose joy is to propose annihilation
of well-tried methods and esprit de corps.
She's cleared her desk. The conference room
is shadowy. The girl she was
would stride the pine woods and bare northern hills
but she has booked retirement leave
among more tangled forest trees
where sun will warm deep pools of gloom
while she unbuttons her profession
to shed it and is glad to rest and weep
until the air cools and it's time to follow
charcoal burners or a witch or speaking owl
and find the magic castle where her life
has all these years been lived by someone else
like her, formidable but fast asleep.

LANDSCAPE WITH PSYCHE

Did heaven shape that heap of wonders
To be the dwelling of a snake?

PIERRE CORNEILLE

Her face is turned away. The sea is there.
The boat from which her sisters call
to urge that she must save herself by murder
is indistinct. So are their voices, shrill
in the quiet afternoon. A buck in line
with her long gaze has grazed for centuries
exactly where he stands. He will not raise
his antlered head to look yet holds in balance
her place and his within the composition.
Her mood is ours. The palace frowns
through carefully assembled trees
but shall admit her. She will listen hard
in shadows on a corner of the stairs
unreached by warm glow from the room he's in
where bottles clink and she can hear a murmur
of satisfied and god-like self-regard.
Sometimes Psyche loves the monster best, sometimes
her handsome man. Each seeks his opposite.
Lust thrives on curiosity. Meanwhile
where are the daylight gleam of precious metal,
the promised pillars and the vaulted roof?
The wallpaper is scuffed. The building shrinks
to somewhere squalid that's not even his.
His motorbike and sidecar block
the ginnel slantwise and his friends squeeze past
rubbing against brick. The loudest
rests his hand against the wall and vomits
as they reach the street. Their quarrelling recedes
and Cupid settles down to drink alone
prodigiously, and for a decent swally
his teeth hinge backwards like a snake.
But this is what she fears not what she sees.
'Sovereign lady, all you see and fear is yours
together with the furies that beset you

with peril and with subterfuge.
Your servants, Ma'am. This is your narrative.
We are your train of ministering voices.
The painting we have found you in seems porous,
capacious, and so fluidly arranged
that it accommodates neglected altars,
envy and the winged bold boy. Your sisters
have left you hesitant. By all means stay
to eavesdrop and to tire your mind and suffer
and then put counsel into execution.
The light is dim. You have a torch
and you may find a sharp knife in the kitchen.'
One step at a time and anxious not to creak
she's coming down and will conceal
her contumacious beauty in a cupboard
underneath the stairs. The slant-parked Zephyr
is also beautiful. Beneath the stars
immortality is an horizon
forever in retreat. His recklessness
makes Cupid almost human. Orders come
from a pillion-creature shrieking shame and rage
provoked by her depleting charms
and ashes of old offerings. Right. Now left.
Turn back. Now right again. Only ourselves
could know her for a goddess in this fettle.
Or him a god despite his winged black leathers.
The air is clean but grabs the throat
like strangler's hands. Direction skids
and wheels turn idly like suspicions
that undermine the heart's felicity
with aftershock among the evening fields
where love sinks under settling dust.
He rights the bike and roars away
the sidecar empty, bashed awry. We dawdle
with prostrate Psyche and her lamentations.
'Dear Madam, you must look for work
assisting ants in warehouses of wheat

and barley, vetches, millet, beans and lentils
for nourishment of sharp-beaked doves of Venus,
or crossing torrents helped by speaking reeds
inspired by river gods and creeping
among the groves to gather golden wool
that clings to bushes and the trunks of trees
from fierce rams that will abide no shepherd.
Endure, and try your hand at anything.'
There's schwingmoor at the edge of Erebus,
a place to linger and to weave
insectivorous and poisonous garlands.
And there's a gate into a field
where mud sucks boots and then a perilous
approach by quivering moss a metre thick
above black depths to where the ferry lands
to take her to beseech of Proserpine
a box of beauty brighter than her own.
She must not open it and yet she does.
A fetid stink hangs in the air. She squelches
through dripping boskage among clawing briars.
She will need cash, for there is greed
even among the dead, and sandwiches
to share with Cerberus. Despite her hurry
she is admiring stalk-stiff bulrushes
whose heads split open every Spring
and fill the air with seeds. A sign:
No Hoping Is Allowed Beyond This Point.
The picture-space we look into contains
all this within a still reality
that rests on artifice. The woods
cohere in huddled colloquy
beneath a listening sky. Cupid's abode
presents a high pillastered front
pierced by unlit windows. The entablature
has obelisks above a balustrade.
Older rounded towers recede. It looms.
It is the setting for what we imagine

is due to Psyche. Whatever happens
will not disturb Claude's contemplative buck
grazing in the seventeenth-century rooms.
He digests myth. He ruminates.
Like him, we're thoughtful and half-close our eyes
to minimise reflected light.
'My lady, you are the bearer of a gift
of beauty from the Queen of Shades herself,
shall you not have the right to dab a smidjin
on your already lovely cheeks and thus
acquire advantage in your husband's eyes?'
She lifts the lid but there is nothing there
except a Stygian fart that drifts
across the pavement out into the traffic.
She slumps on tarmac and inhales
erasure of her senses. This is death
if Cupid will not come on dewy wings
with ringlets on his neck and snowy brow
to gather up her sleep and close the box.
And how would Soul then couple with Desire?
Her sisters rent a place where every night
consists of living for the day.
We take a taxi through an inner-city
to find their clothes-strewn flat-share and a glass
or three of hooch. News of her dire misfortune
delights them privily for now
they scheme that Cupid will choose one of them.
Each by herself next groggy morning heads
homeward, though not to Mum and Dad, bereft
of Psyche in their close-shut house,
but to an eyrie near the peak
of Kawasaki, crying out to Zephyr
to bear them in their glad-rags to his lord.
They are swept up bodily but not sustained
above the precipice to which their spite
and envy took them to be dashed to pieces.
The seasons crimson all things with their roses.

No one winds the clocks on Mount Olympus.
Cupid and Psyche's special day
has no beginning and no end. The party
swings forever. The gods are there.
They've trashed the place and revellers
spill into the street. The police
are on their way eternally.
Floorboards are ripped up. Walls are kicked and scratched.
The music is unbearable.
Carvings and paintings representing beasts
of the chase and rustic scenes adapted
to please the eye are shamefully defaced.
The state apartments have been wrecked.
Jewellery and rare productions
of craftsmanship and nature all together
with sumptuous hangings have gone walkabout.
A knife is missing from a kitchen drawer.
Neighbours in Arcadia have been assured
that grief like this gets zero-tolerance.
But round here it's still tough mythology.
'Madam, let's slip away from such shenanigans
to Cupid's halls, where you shall reign
though mortal as immortal queen.
Your manly god will not at all resemble
a loathsome serpent but a comely youth
who's on the wagon now. The bike is sold.
There is no call for murder and his mother
condescends to visit. We, your faithful train
of voices, croak. As we grow old
enjoyments and refinements mellow us.'
In a chamber with a view beyond the sea
through painted trees into a hushed museum,
ages away yet near, where connoisseurs
pause among undisputed masterworks
savouring the smell of polish,
our afternoon is witnessing
the birth of Pleasure. She is our child too.

All is resolved. The buck lifts up his head
and Venus remounts her throne. Her altars glow.
Psyche warms to nectar and ambrosia
but will not claim comparison
with She, fountain of elements.
That's all that we remember. Paparazzi
flash pictures of her as a butterfly.
The heavenly assembly drinks a toast
to perpetuity. We echo it.
While those below, who could not help but kiss
their fingertips at sight of her,
forget and are themselves in time forgotten,
the gods refresh their taste for human beauty.

Proxy

Stay here and be myself but sick and old,
the wreck of me, my Brother Ass
spavined and irresolute. I've set you down
in a courtyard with wisteria
and darkening lemon leaves and water play.
White houses and a church comprise the town
with shallow roofs and storks' nests. We have seen,
as we approached, the sweep of bay
towards the cliff and have discussed
distant pallid mainland and the golden
hem of the horizon and the ocean
acting blue for us. My friend, this is the crust
on the pie of suffering. Tuck in.
I wish you well. Goodbye. I'm young again.

Next Time

Church-smell holds my breath. There is a flutter
high in the roof as if the Holy Ghost
embodied by a bird has lost Her way
between a moment and its memory.
A spider crossing in an eightsome skelter
blood-glow of stained glass did so already.
My time is dwindling but I can't adjust
to squeeze myself into a smaller future
while *That was now* and *This is then* are twisting
recall and attention out of kilter.
The fluttering has reached my head. The spider
has found its way again to unlit dust.
Cool stillness is complete, a silence bruised
and waiting till I come back yesterday.

After Pevsner

To appreciate the house it must be seen
in the radiance emitted by its own
baroque bravura and immensity.
Although the hills are softened by plantation
the contrast with surrounding barrenness
shocks each time it shows itself so that our eyes
are locked until they are released
to strain again to watch it fade from view.
As someone said, in fact a novelist:
'It is as if I'm shown a masterpiece
secreted in a grotto, or a statue
of a goddess in her splendour in a barn.'
No one can get there easily or soon.
The heights of its estates command the passes.

Pastoral

(for Alistair Elliot)

Wherever I can find a meadow, ghosts
of mowers move in line like handwriting
across grass readied for the scythe by dew.
I'm shadowing their shadows, on their heels
and in their balance and their rhythm breathing
to stride into the cut and tug a string
tight to stop a frightened vole from running
up a trouser leg. There's laughter here and song
exactly at the moment of its loss.
And I shall loiter among sheaves
to drink the peace they leave, the purple glow
when they go home down lanes and into graves.
I'm aftermath, foggage and bullimong,
an upstart in the poetry of fields.

Virgil

Bright sunshine will distort what it reveals.
Politicians like the light. We're strung along.
This afternoon I rubbed my thumb
around the chipped rim of a coffee cup
and thought what could be worse. A shining gulf
might be decreed, dividing day from night.
Penumbra though, which public glare conceals,
will long outlast deceit and pelf.
At work there is the genius by whom
gloaming was first written down. The shepherd youth
Nostalgia, arm in arm with sister Hiraeth,
is with him and still prompts him into song
in groves where milk-white peacocks droop
their ghostly tails and squawk the truth.

French Windows

The folly tower you noticed from the train
and thought of for the rest of one short journey
when you were young is where I choose to linger.
On all your birthdays I unfurl a banner
above the decorative battlements.
I do not age. I don't forget.
Once there were people here. They went away
through tall French windows borrowed from the set
of some old-fashioned comedy
and left behind a well-found elegance.
The place is nowhere that a connoisseur
would classify as an essential structure
but stands its ground with dignity.
It would have suited you. Where have you been?

Sanquar

The good man pauses as if in a frame
between the gatepiers of the cemetery –
corniced, and each topped with a pyramid –
and looks apologetically
regretful that I've spotted him.
He comes to make sure that the dead
sleep tight beneath the stone of Rachel Hair,
together with her child. Both died
to save his life once in a brawl
with Cromwell's Ironsides. It's in the form
of two adjoining coffins, big and small.
As if he were to blame for history,
the good man haunts the town each night in shame
because he is not buried with them there.

LADDEREDGE AND COTISLEA

We thought we were living now,
but we were living then.

ANNE STEVENSON

Towards the farm at which I am permitted
inside the barn and then to climb the hay bales
is an old man with a scythe says Youngster
unwrapping as I skip to greet him sacking
from the blade. He slides the stone along
long time. I think I see my mother's hand
withdrawn from drawing curtains at a window
slip back into that room with the aroma
of nearly damp encyclopaedias.
Mind can touch mind. I feel my tongue
begin to press the past. The box
that sits on the table called Occasional
her fingers rest upon has mirrored drawers
whose memories are asking me to speak.
The chimney whispers to the clean cold hearth.

The brave boys that have gone away
will march back home one sunny day.

You can't get what you need for love nor money.
I do not understand how that it is
the opposite direction for the lane
will join the road towards a future farther
than Buxton is or Macclesfield and people
After the War Before the War
are selling what they do to live. It's called
the World of Work. It's in a dream
I hear them talk. I'm half awake.
What can you do? There aren't the men.
There is a doll to be undressed
and school books of my uncles who are dead
but aren't dead now of course but are Called Up
like Daddy who I don't know yet.
It seems you have an interest in silence

and oily dust where nothing is disturbed
in which case you will want to hear
about an Austin Seven up on blocks
behind its blistered garage doors
and petrol rations. There's a fox
all night in Mollock's Wood. I think he tries
to sing to me. I am asleep.

And with the big girls in the gorse
who tell things and play Truth Or Dare or worse.

Caterpillar Tractor is the best thing.
Milk Cart though comes every morning
with that horse has a name that I can say
but I don't know it now. The dippers clatter
with different voices and are big and little
to lift milk from the churn. Someone is laughing.
The same hand from the curtains holds the jug.
I paint an outhouse door with Dolly Blue
which makes it wet not blue. Another fox
I think sings like the one I know at night
up on the roof the wind turns. Later a pond
has a spit where I will dig a grave
among the tree roots where I know
it is the best place for a Viking cat.
As well in future I will have my bus fare
to where the vet lives and back with her dead.
That place will also be where Harvey
shows us his Circumcision. Up the lane
the cows come which have heavy tails.
I stalk them in my wellingtons.

Another laugh. Jam Rags on the line. A shout.
Toys in a van. Demobbed. The air is soot.

The ceiling light hangs like a chandelier
with fitments where gas mantles were
and has a middle that's a crown.
It has to go and crashes. I will try
to wear it in a cloud of dust.
Daddy is hammering. Outside air is clean.
At night I shall not hear the fox.
But in the day is Blow Lamp. Paint comes off.
Even Lincrusta. The house is old
and has a cellar but will be like new.
The curtains are not wide enough.
Hands will bring poppers that will keep them shut
and rise to stitch against the sun.
The house is in a marl field. That means clay.
And where the pond is it is like a lake.
The Viking sea. I have a Siren Suit
and talk to grown-up children at the gate
when street lights being lit. I think I've come
a long way off and they don't like my name.

It's nearly Christmas what it is. I wake
in time for Daddy's Home Now motorbike.

The bully has a needle with a hilt
like a sword. It is a hat pin.
He is the torturer outside the outside
lavatory. He shall stay where air is soot.
I'll make a notice for a Zoo and tie it
big to the garden gate. No one will come.
There's just the goldfish and the toad
that's always in the coal-shed but today
is not. I do not know what's true when that is
but you will know by now. We're on a Walk.
Mummy that's the hands and Daddy
and pushchair Margaret. I find butter
in fresh packets hid behind a tree beside
the path where no one lives. It is Black Market

166

so we will take it home and not
Waste Time Worrying. Another day
we hear a voice that shouts *A Murrain On Ye*
at us from a bleak barn with an echo.

Christmas occurs and Santa Claus
and tears and frightening said and slamming doors.

There is a worse dream or maybe a part
that happens on its own and seems
more anxious. There are lavatories again
but this time made by sculptors out of junk
like driftwood with some paint adhering, toys
and car parts and with various containers.
Some are stuck up in the air and shaky
and some are squelchy underground.
The creatures that are queueing see right in.
They don't know me. Though some are nice
most are indifferent and grunt
or if they seem like women they will sigh.
I should have something that I do to sell
but all I've got is words they grab
and look at upside down. It is the World
of Work. They cannot read but like to feel
the paper. Martin lives in a Council House.
His Dad has a shed with tools. One day he lets
us have a log and hammers and a bag
of panel pins. We knock them in
and trying not to bend them till the log
is heavy Heaven with a thousand stars.

You only need to blink to think
about me and the years between us shrink.

The Tip is where we go along the track
out into fields by Whittle's shop.
You smell it burning and not breathing parts
are sticky hot. That's where we find what treasure
is to play with. There are gas masks and helmets
and sometimes German ones and bayonets
and bicycles to put together bits.
There's a story that's got me in it before
all that which Mummy tells she laughs about.
Perhaps you'll laugh as well for listening.
The Combine Harvester has stopped
and waits and tucks its shadow in. It's time
for sandwiches and lemonade
but there are men with guns around the island
that is still standing crop. I hear the rustle
of the rabbits very frightened and the hares
as well there with me and the shotgun barrels
click into place. What happens is
that my red hat and me are glimpsed
in one small movement of the corn.
The guns are lowered and the air is heavy
and by my movement and because that moment
I shall live as long as you exactly.
Mummy what are you thinking of
or chatting to a Land Girl without thought?
There is another Walk and when it's frosty
so Magic Lane is pink because the sky
and there are clouds shaped like a T
because it's Time for Tea which Daddy says.
I race him home. He lets me win.

Who has a mo-mo off the Tip?
Whose little mo-mo says Pip Pip?

Up the road I must not where are different
children is a pumping station
abandoned with a bashed-in door
with old machinery and rust
and knee-deep water trouble happens with.
The different children Mummy says are Rough.
This summer there is hidden grass
between the clumps of gorse up at the top
of Back Field where the big girls are
that show their knickers. It's tea-time again
but late and Daddy in the distance looking.
Uncle George is not my uncle
but Mr Gibson who makes cider
drip through straw that smell I like.
One day I shall say odoriferous
and sesquipedalian for you too.
He saws a Walking Stick be short for me.
Now when the sun keeps still I go
down in the big weeds living in his garden
to where it's warming at a wall where once
upon a time he tied an Animal.
It has an iron ring that hangs
to put my nose in that's still low enough
for me wherever it has gone to now.

Pig in the book has nose that has a ring
so ring has nose will be a funny thing.

But in another dream my head slides through
and then I see it. I am on my own
more frightened now than ever I remember
and footsteps on the landing in the night
until I pay attention. What I say
even in the sun that's in the garden
or in the wood where foxes sing
goes to a dark mask in a circular
hat shape that's huge and is an ear as well

and like the inside of a black umbrella.
But it will also go to you-that's-me –
an old man in an armchair looking back.
The other fox does not turn in the wind
above my bed but on a different roof
on Woodside Lane one day he winks
when Mummy *Look At Fox* and lifts me up.
The work that is the world is time.

Daddy will crank my bed into a car.
I drive to sleep. He did not like the War.

Down the road there is a Bottling Machine
and Sour that is the bad smell. Mr Clayton
brings milk with a Milk Float now and has no horse
but Ferrets that want all the time to eat
my fingers. I'm putting off the worst thing.
This summer too is time for Dens
in Coppice Wood and Mollock's Wood to hide
and hunt and find the others first.
I have forgotten home is where-am-I
once more when Daddy worried so of course
it's not the first occasion or the last
and it is not the worst thing which is what
it is that only happens once for ever.
In due course we shall come to that.
Biffs to the head will cause imagination.
But Mummy says I worry him too much
about me that I'll worry him to death.

I've watched my father reach for breath and die.
I'm reading Biggles. Boys don't cry.

I see the place he used to hang
his leather Crash Hat and his Goggles
are hidden somewhere what I think
and Gauntlets gone were on the kitchen chair.
But may I still go out to play?
September's coming and with engines chewing
fog and steam and smoke and fire and hauling
vacant carriages with sepia photographs
and luggage racks like fishing nets and me
along the soon closed Churnet Valley Line
to stop at Rudyard Lake, Cliffe Park and Rushton,
Bosley Halt, North Rode and Macclesfield.
And School. But that is always afterwards.
There's also in this summer time for jousting
on bikes with six foot garden canes
from Firth's the shop for everything.
The aim is not to stick an eye
and that could happen but to get the lance
between the spokes and throw him off.
We all have proper shields not dustbin lids
and helmets from the Tip to beat each other
with heavy sticks. It is the Middle Ages
and violent and innocent.
But there is Keith from Sunday School
too old for us who comes to show us fireworks
kept back from Bonfire Night and mice
and frogs blown up and what he does
to insects that have wings and legs.
He has a girlfriend too and tells us what
she does that's what he makes her do.
On a lawn by Woodside Lane a mower leaves
the smell that is the panic of the grass.

I think you think that what I say is Now
which means that I am nearly you.

I'm down among the dreams again and dreaming
about the big black hat that is the ear
of sleep and voices that I love the most
go silent there for ever and inside it –
Greased Lightning gone as quick as that –
and also of the mirror box
that falls from the table called Occasional
and shatters me awake. Footsteps come and hands
at night in August half-light by the marl field.
It doesn't really break. My face looks back
at me-that's-you from every drawer
but something is that sort happening she says
and pulls beside herself and me to Daddy.
We are too proud to have The Telephone
and can't afford it anyway
so she has gone to rouse them at the Dairy
but I can watch him and I always shall
where it is almost dawn and hear him breathe
like slow strokes of the stone along
long time and loud then sudden louder stop.
The scythe is sharp and I think Good.

I sold the world a life for time to do
this work for nothing, finding words for True.

The Gypsy Fiddle

The garden wall is higher than two men
but he is free to roam the lawn
as if it were a world. He greets the day
with a shrill aubade and spreads his palms to swear
the oath that binds him never to disclose
the secrets of his race or teach the cant
to dommerars or patricoes,
abrams, Irish toyles or clapperdogeons
and always to share out in fellowship
what he can steal from libkins or the ruffmans
while cleaving stiffly to a doxy wap.
He'll bring her duds, tibs of the buttery,
margery praters, grunting cheats,
as winnings for her weppings. As if their rags
were ropes to tie them they will be as one
in all the thievings he imagines.
His lamentations are heartfelt and subtle
and he can grip a tune. Although he eats
more like a beast than human creature
and has no ready ribbin he'll not want
for peckage. The light fades. He has earned a nap.
Beside the rockery a deck chair sags
where he is resting like a gypsy fiddle
from which the bow has been withdrawn.

The Vapour Trail

On the west side of the room there is a set
of three large windows. It will be
perhaps her favourite spot. It's getting dark
but she remains preoccupied
by what she felt at sunset when she looked
above the looming shrubbery
to see a vapour trail light up, blood-red,
and cut the sky. She drops her coat
across a packing-case and flicks
the light switch as she wonders where to start.
It's best, she has been told – the first
time sweeping any house – that it's done *inward*,
so good luck isn't lost like dust.
But memories, she thinks, should be swept *out*
with all their hurt. Then check each door is locked.

Death and the Spinster

The problem is, now I'm alone and old,
that mirrors also start to age and tarnish.
Tonight let's look in one of them together
and ponder our proximity.
Press up tight behind my shoulder.
I will do my best to focus
on each of us in turn until I'm sure
we've got a clear joint-portrait in reverse.
Don't think I'm fostering a tenderness
for the grotesque. I dread the day
when all reflections lose themselves for ever
among the flaws and whorls of antique glass.
Even now, fine crazing and pale mustard-brown
discolourations spread out to obscure
the features I'm most eager to behold –
my blushing cheeks, your smile of bone,
the fondness that is evident between us –
and I forget how beautiful we are.

My Mother at Erbistock

The river is and carries off the rain
that came with summer thunder in the heart
of Wales to England and the sands of Dee.
A butterfly, where beech roots sieve the flow
falls upwards through the rungs of air.
You would have noticed it and told its name.
White noise incessant on the weir
drowns children's laughter happy in the day
before their futures start. To call us home,
to call us home with every memory
and all that love you had for time
when family coheres is what you do.
Down where the bank is shallower
swallows slip anchor in reflected blue.
I'm still your child that was. Hold tight my arm.
We'll wade together now and turn the sky
once more to ripples of the brown flood water.

A Piano in Hobart

(for Michael and François)

If tuning turns out to be difficult
the fault most often lies in weaknesses
and instabilities. Lest we forget,
now we begin to walk and talk, the thin
memorial flame becomes more visible
as sunlit dazzle yields to spats of rain.
The grass has recently been mown.
Sometimes the soundboard's curvature
together with the angle of a string
become exaggerated and display
crucial points most under pressure
from struggles with the tension of the steel
towards best pitch. The estuary
is broadening beyond the cenotaph
in order to become the sea.
Each string bears eighty kilograms of stress.
That's twenty tonnes. The metal frame
is made to stiffen the harmonic structure
but not constrict the breath of sound.
Mount Wellington pulls down the cloud. Up there
Spring weather has not yet arrived.
Two world wars are commemorated here
together with Korea and Malaya,
Indonesia and Vietnam
and lives mislaid away from home.
The layered wood and metal of the wrestplank
is also subject to intense
and searing pressure. Birdsong for a moment
is drawing out a wine cork squeakily
unlike the wood grain of the resonator
which is compressed so pulsing qualities,
in step with melody and harmony
and their affinities, are amplified

before transmission to the ear. This morning
we're at the birthplace of Van Diemen's Land.
Brass studs set in the pavement mark the route
the causeway took like an umbilicus.
Mother ships moored off the isthmus nourished
trade and settlement. Here is the School of Art.
In time a wrestplank can succumb to bending
and tip forward. Its pin housings,
affected by repeated chords,
becoming oval in severest cases.
The pins themselves may fail, worn out and rusted.
And here's the Institute of Engineering
in Tudor style but with a roof
of corrugated iron and a pole
to fly a flag which strains the rope. Rotations
repeated frequently make screw threads dull.
It's pleasanter to listen to ourselves
in cities we may never see again
although we hope. This ambling chat
revives young aspirations. Fully loaded,
strings must hold at their required tension
without detachment of the soundboard ribs.
The Drunken Admiral is closed
to thirsty brawlers, disembarked
two hundred years ago. Piano wire,
rail tracks and corrugated came
ashore from Hunter Island on the strength
of sailors and convicted men. Remember
that all adjustment has an influence,
even when meticulous and limited
to one part only, on the entire thing.
The Quarantine Shed stood where a building site
promises residential luxury
but there or anywhere disintegration
will come at last to a pianoforte
or any many-layered construction
be it an instrument of art and pleasure,

of comprehension, or of memory,
and also make an end of who we are
dans cette vie. Merci, François. Thank you, Michael.
Fountain water breezes sideways
to kiss our faces as we turn toward
Salamanca one last time. Old tuners dread
the snap of tarnished strings grown stiff with age,
and old geographers intuited
the Southern continents because they knew
without them that the world would topple over
becoming music we will never hear.

NAYLER

Not many rich nor many wise
doe come to know these things.

MARTHA SIMMONS

I

On hills where winds are sharp and several,
tooth-houses, hollow to the root,
preserve a comfortable ache
recalling glow in hearths. Stone walls
hold warmth into the winter if you press
your back against them, and breathe small
an' woo that fair mountain nymph, sweet Liberty.
Find one that has a roof and live in it.

II

Reverberations among graves
enhance the quietness when it returns
as if the traffic brings about
intermittent prayerful hush. This instant now
in sunlight of four centuries
I see a mare and foal disturbed
while grazing, as my dog barks poetry
as best he can to urge me – gateward-bound
not knowing whither – to decline
to give up my estate, cast out my money
and witness to redemption from the world.
They shrug themselves from reverie
and lift their heads to see me turn
my face away from my own fields.
St Mary Woodkirk is engaged with God
in its churchyard on the Leeds to Dewsbury road.
The doors are locked. It is the truth
I hear in my own voice that makes me tremble,
and I'm no more a member of that sweet
society, that seeking church.
Our adversary must deploy his wiles
and there is beating of the air
in trusting to a metaphor.

If you are doubtful stop your ears
and do not look me in the eye. Or else
abide while patience brings us clarity.
The plough I left embedded in its furrow
becomes a tongue to till men's minds.
What's sown in light and life will yield
apocatastesis from heavy marl.

III

I understand you, James. I'll drink to that.
Your words have reached me where the Wansbeck rises
on the wild hills o' Wannys far, far away,
and north of the gloving town of Hexham, north
of Hadrian's Wall and of the Tone Pit Inn,
in time which is to you unborn. A place
where England is debatable and swallows
come back from Africa – each less in weight
than this filled fountain pen – to nest inside
the porch above the door I use on tiptoe
about my business with the generator,
the mower, drain-rods in their fascist bundle,
until each brood has hatched and fledged and flown.
Shadows overlap in deeper shadow.
James, *my gostly fader*, my confessor,
each time you speak I also hear another.
My real father died while he was young.
And I was young then too. But I remember.

IV

Friend, in tenderness of heart I am aware
of your location and of how you ettle,
bound in wedlock to mundane creation.
That which will cleanse corrupt things from the vessel
shall prevail. Meanwhile I'm ready in your mind
to share its restless pleasure, for example
in witnessing seduction of the bees
on summer afternoons. Lewd openness
there is of foxgloves. Thus the world
sets out to capture us, its richnesses
apparent every time we rediscover
close attention. Yes, in worship also.
I am entangling your circumstances
in all I recollect of mine, and you
are tolerant, because you think I see
a short cut to the place whereat to enter
life entirely. And you listen.
In being heard I find my zeal rekindled.
I preach the Kingdom – undefiled
and never to be done away –
with voice refreshed. I'm not deceived
by the know-it-all you seem to like to seem,
proclaiming that it's not too late to learn,
consulting flesh and blood as you look round
complacently, and risk your soul
where wilderness and darkness wait. What's more,
I recognise discipleship, beside
that pine plantation in the Wilds of Wanney,
and aptitude, and thirst for truth
that gulps my words down with the rain
which smells of wet trees and of distances.

V

Sit thee under thine own vine, to feed in peace.
Stories addle through containment,
so I will tell you in our own good time
all that befell, imperfectly
but truthfully, if inexact,
and ask you to come with me as I go
engaged upon this work that's ours yet other.
Diligently hearken me. There came a day
at Ardsley, after nine years making war,
when I was quartermaster under Lambert
in the army of the saints, and on that day
delight and fullness inexhaustible.
The sky was flame and in it lightning. Creatures
flew from it shining, as did those
Ezekiel saw, and then flew back
to be refreshed by fire and every one
straight forward. Whither the spirit was to go
they went, and turned not when they went,
and from that time I knew that so must I.

VI

Apologies. I am preoccupied.
So clear a dream. I meet him off the train.
His mackintosh is damp, his hat pulled down.
He speaks to me. His son. I fall awake.
An' listen the lapwing and lonely curlew.
They question sleep. But morning stalls, delays
acceptance of a moorland shape,
delays the hearth's assertion of a flame,
the heart's assertion of the will,
and daylight, dragged on with my clothes. He's gone.
This time he nearly told me where he'd been.

VII

I'll start again. Yes, from that time on I knew
that so must I. God summoned me –
which was the God I learned of as a child
but had not recognised – and I,
intent to overcome the world,
at barley seed time of the year
came forth from Yorkshire, north and west,
foot-sore and saddle-sore by Windermere,
taking days and nights about it.
George welcomed me, as you do now,
and all that summer strove in disputation
with William Lampitt, vicar of Ulverston,
a high notionist, a Ranter in his mind,
denouncing him in his own church.
'George Fox,' cried out the magistrates
and captains to Judge Thomas Fell,
as he rode home across the sands
of Morecambe Bay, 'George Fox it is, George Fox
bewitches people out of their religion
and Mistress Fell for one. All quake.'
Their horses jostled as they smelled the tide.
When Margaret Fell herself discerned that priest,
convincement of the Lord's truth came upon her
and furthermore upon her family.

VIII

Yes I'll come with you, James, and wear the shoes
in which the two of us can walk together
among the places you bore witness in.
And let's start here, where Swarthmoor Hall
is seemly in grey rendering,
and gardens shimmer. It is warm late June.

Windows with leaded diamond panes
are gripped by mullions, grey stone on grey,
smaller, and more irregularly set
than might be pleasing to more careful taste.
This house was never built for that.
Dismantled piecemeal, piecemeal re-erected,
convulsing slowly from within,
it has been added to and taken from
to satisfy each new decade and lustrum,
enduring anyhow, creating puzzles
for archaeologists and gaining height
without elegance, contriving
to leave a four-post newel, one of three
thought to exist, short of the roof
it was intended to support. Explore.
Lift pewter tableware to guess its weight
and lightly touch, as if for luck,
the chair in which John Woolman died:
'So near to death that I forgot my name,
I prayed to know it and was shown a mass
of dull and gloomy matter filling up
a quarter of the world and it was formed
by human creatures in as great a misery
as they could bear yet live and I was mixed
in with it and was not distinct, and then
a voice more pure than ever heard announced
the death within myself of my own will.'
Your words or very like them, John,
and spoken silently by your armchair.
Despite exposure to the aforementioned
sunlight of four centuries, the battering
of bitter weather, this estate
is well kept-up, its ambience intact.
Friends are moved to contribute financially
that a pure fear be preserved in them. *Enjoy*
your visit, trusting if thou knowest it
the eye that never changes, and stand single.

Be not lifted up above thy measure
but yet delight thyself. Breathe in
the airs and scents of this six score of acres
close to the heart of Cumbria,
which heart was beating then in Cumberland.
The grass-mown labyrinth is overgrown
and hard to trace. Instead, we'll take
the broad path to the bottom of the meadow
and find the beehives, where our interest
will prompt the bees to keep their obligations
airborne among woundwort, plantain, knapweed,
bird's foot trefoil, buttercup and bugle.
The foxgloves flaunt beside the sun-warmed wall
that guides us back to where a gang
of chimneys indicates the house.
We're in the office during working hours.
If we can help in any way,
just say the word. And don't forget,
your entry fee includes the audio tour!

IX

How art thou found, now that the Light is risen?
The sun shines on the Wanneys too. Which summer
this is the last warm day of I'm not sure.
It's memory. Instructions to myself:
Sprawl in a garden chair. Grin at the dazzle.
Embrace the heat. When it turns cloudy, walk
to the tarn beside Aid Crag and watch the mist
bloom like dry ice. Wait to witness
what happens on the platform of the water
until the sky begins to darken. Start
a deer as you shove home through the plantation.
There will be music round your head. The birds
have seized the same fine day as you and sing it.
They'll not remember. You will, though.

189

X

Goodbye to Swarthmoor. We've already come
to Barrow, where the great Dock Hall
looms above the roofs of shipyard workers.
This is the home town of the glamour boats,
the Navy's hunt-kill submarines,
wherefrom the Spearfish and the Tomahawk
proffer with slaughter what belongs with slaughter –
light wounding, step by step to grievous maiming,
bereavement, pain beyond endurance, madness,
fouled innocence, the beating down of art –
accurately to a metre
across a thousand miles of land and ocean.
Therefore, brethren, in the Light be faithful
which hides from that which feeds on earthly things.
Fair Seas, *Astute* and *Ambush*, and Bravo
to *Artful* and *Audacious*. Good Luck *Anson*,
Agincourt and *Agamemnon*.
May Rolls-Royce warm your nuclear hearts,
secure inside ceramic vests, comprising
numberless accoustic tiles, that hinder
recognition of your menace
as you submerge to work in sonic shimmer.
In this condition thou shalt find no peace.

XI

And Bravo to the man who called us out
from the meeting that we held, with one convinced,
down the road at Cockan, that his pistol
snapped in our faces but did not go off,
and afterwards that he was struck
by the power of the Lord and hid himself
and trembled in a cellar. Again, Bravo

to forty more, with staves and clubs,
muckforks, flails and fishing poles, that fell
upon us when we came to Walney Island,
striking, punching, endeavouring to thrust
us back into the sea, and poor George mazed
and coming to himself to find a woman
pelting him with stones, her husband
kneeling atop of him to keep them off.
Do not think it strange, the nearer that you draw
to He who brings you victory,
that you sink deeper into tribulation
and sufferings increase upon the fleshly part.
His will is all. When at last a horse was sent,
I could not bear its shaking for much pain.

XII

Run not with that which is in haste.
Days are shortening, in time unborn. Yet still
horizons to the west will not recede,
but crowd my open gate. The air is clean
and chilly. From my garden chair –
defiant on the drive between the gateposts –
I'm holding them at bay with bursts
of Verdi, from my ghetto-blaster. Heather
is ablaze on Berry Crag and Callerhues.
A snake of fire tugs at a drift
of distant smoke, and there is no one now
on afternoons like this to sit with me.
No one is welcome. Yevtushenko wrote:
'Cheer up. Yours is no unique condition.'

XIII

Indeed. At Lancaster, the quarter sessions
can prove no blasphemy. The priests
have great consulting, and their conclaves
send all the country hereabouts
abroad for witnesses, to speak
against us. They demand at every turn
to know if Christ be in me, as a man,
because they dare to preach Christ is in Heaven,
and with a carnal body. I proclaim
that Christ is not divided. If He be,
He is no longer Christ. I witness
Christ in me, and God in man, in measure.
That England should not lack for entertainment,
last week they took my hat off with a pitchfork
while we debated in a field,
but I still have it, God be praised.
When Francis Howgill that was with us, speaking
with mighty power, though all the people raged,
was brought before the magistrates,
his hat was thrown into the fire.
I say again, Christ filleth earth and Heaven,
and is not carnal but in spirit. That He
should be in heaven, and in flesh and blood,
beside the saints with spiritual bodies
is not proportionable. Canst thou believe
it was a carnal body that came in,
as John relates, not once but twice,
where the disciples were, the door being shut?
Christ is a mystery. They know Him not.
Although he made it clear what I should do,
most civilly, I would not bare my head
before a justice of the peace
in the alehouse on the road from Orton,
and did address that suave and equal man
as 'Thou'. They have their writ of *mittimus*.

XIV

Tractors hauling livestock, hay bales
and agricultural machinery,
swerve out from the market square of Appleby,
queen of the towns of Westmorland,
and squeeze themselves through tightening history
to pass beneath a vanished gaol,
vibrating as the Eden swells,
within the gatehouse of an erstwhile bridge
where I lie dwindling on bread and water
and in this January have no fire.
St Mary Woodkirk, disengaged with God,
has excommunicated me. And always
an earthly and adulterous spirit prowls,
determined to devour the precious life
and tie the soul to things below.
But Anne, my wife, has been and I enjoyed
great refreshment by her coming.
And Margaret Fell, in God's name, sent two pounds.
Each day they ask again, is Christ in thee?

XV

In that which has proved liberty stand fast.
Today I dig up and enjoy
broad-shouldered radishes. Home grown.
And they are flavourful and good.
This bucks me up and I set off to ramble,
late in the day, and lightly dressed. The last
excitement of the sky burns out and rain
leans down as night falls on a clueless stumble.
I'm lost. Is it too late in life, in any case,
to find my way back home and close the door?
God maketh all things new, both earth and heaven,

and also a new man to walk
therein with cheerfulness, as bonds are loosed.

XVI

Dawn breaks above the town. And crump.
I wake up shaken by a labouring cough.
And crump. And crump. A pile driver whacks the ground
behind the churchyard at St Lawrence's,
where flood-stained pews reveal the heights
the river reaches. Come next cricket season,
a new pavilion will stand on concrete stilts.
Meanwhile, I am more easefully confined,
adjacent to the gaol. The gaoler's wife
is tender to the truth. Once as a girl
she saw that wonderful surprising oak,
in Whinfield Forest hereabouts, they call
the Brethren Tree, last of three ancient brothers,
and tells how big it was, how on
the north-east side, next Temple Sowerby,
there was an entrance broke out as a doorway
where people might walk in, or ride
on horseback, strange as that may seem.
The inward prospect, so she says, resembled
some ruined tower, dismally decayed,
and in the cavities therein were bats.
What moves my heart is that she still remembers,
up high, one twig alone with green leaves on it.
How like that is to my unique condition.
And yours, Yevgeny. And to yours.

XVII

Well, I should wake up too, and get things done.
The tank, above the ceiling of the kitchen,
that takes the rain that smells of distances
straight from the gutter has run low,
and if I'm going to make a cup of tea,
here in my windswept elsewhere time,
I must walk over to the spring –
across the fell, and in among the pines –
with a plastic jerry-can, already stained,
as you can see, by iron in the water.
I'm neat in my own company. And yet
however long I am alone, it's still
as if I've just arrived. The house is full
of boxes of a life I'm rooting through
in order to discover who,
however odd or long ago it seems,
is packed in them. While past and present seek
incorporation, things will wait
to be re-recognised and juxtaposed
till I decide what's useful and what for.

XVIII

Yes James, I'm back, and catching up.
You tell me that iniquity has grown
to such an height that none should come to London
but those raised in pure movings of the truth,
for in this city is the Serpent's wisdom
grown fully ripe. And yet we're here.
The driver leans out from his cab to shout
that he has been instructed that the bus
must wait, three stops before our destination,
to even-out the service. Now he slumps

and so do we. Ministration of the world
is that of man, and doth not lead
to any end. We live in time, however,
and time itself must have an end,
for it is not of God. The Bull and Mouth
with its resounding stable-yard,
in which the word that shall abide was preached,
has sunk, with Aldersgate itself,
among the potsherds, oyster shells and ashes
of the dreadful burning of the City.
Yet echoes persist of what was promised here,
even everlastingly, that wranglings,
and persecutions in those days,
could never overpower, nor thoroughfares
that deafen now. The city shrugs.
In earshot of those murmurs, there are meetings
on summer afternoons, in open air
and of a Christian kind. And it was here
that Wesley felt his heart be warmed,
and salvaged from the law of sin and death.
All such occurrences, God knows, are one.

XIX

The dark ravens bield on thy grey cliffs sae hie.
Tonight, Northumberland is strafed
by crazing gusts. The blackness lives.
Leaves, bracken, straw, small animals,
flit and swivel in my homesick headlights.
A horse rears up in front of me.
Signposts are turned and trees blown down.
It's home. I'll have no other. Raw winds roar.

XX

As soon as we are off again, the bus
accelerates into a stop,
and there are terrifying roads to cross
towards an unexpected nook, among
the concrete walkways of the Barbican,
and resolution in surprise. *Ye Gods,*
what a glorious twist: a bull, a mouth
engulfing it, and pipe-smoke clouds
like pineapples, and verse on a cartouche
concerning Milo of Croton, who once decked
an ox with one blow of his wrestler's *fist*
and ate it whole. Oh dear. Rhyme calls for rhyme
that does not make us curl our toes
when chiselled into stone, but moves
us forward in obliquity,
aesthetically reassured.
I stole a cosse of grete swetenesse,
but I restore it shall doutless.
John Greenleaf Whittier, the Quaker poet
quietly at home between his pages,
spine by spine with Watkins, Whitman, Williams,
writes of his Conductor Bradley,
'others he saved, himself he could not save';
and not facetiously, as we are told
that priests and thieves and scribes and elders mocked
our Saviour, but with respect
for duty done. Since Martha Simmonds set
me up so high in her imaginings,
I have been learning humbleness.
We are in Postman's Park – a stroll
away through traffic from the mighty throat
of our Crotonian – to think
on more reminders of self-sacrifice
and further likenesses of my condition:
Solomon Galaman, eleven years old,

when his small brother strayed among the wheels
and sharp hooves of Commercial Street.
'Mother, I saved him but.' So long ago.
More worthy him by far than I.
'*Your* mother is now Martha,' so quips George.

XXI

Timepiece, Exeter's half-decent nightclub,
near Rougemont Gardens, in the old-town quarter,
disturbs the peace of unborn time
with shocks of bass and ultraviolet light
and stimulates oblivion
here in the same space as this tomb
for living men. Behold your quartermaster
in gaol again. A vagabond.
O let my shining be in the right nature
and my rising be as I am born of God.
Yes George, it's true that something was got up
in me against thee, that I warned
thee, there on Little Castle Street, to take
less heed of lying or of false accusings
made of me. And many heard. But dids't thou not
come later to the prison, threatening,
condemning me as one gone from the truth,
and also tempting me with promises
if I would bow down in obedience?
Where I, and company you have called rude –
yes, and even filthy spirits –
were waiting, was set down below
the main part of the chamber. You'll remember.
I held an apple up for you and wept,
entreating: 'If I have favour in thy sight
receive.' How cold was your demeanour then:
'If thou canst say that thou art moved
by the Lord to give it me I shall.' Oh George!

I said, 'so would you have me lie?'
and reached up to embrace you, but you would not
bend or clamber down, but offered me your hand
and then your foot to kiss. Though there remains
still love enough to draw me back to you
through fire and water, I am made to look
beyond all man for comfort. Farewell brother.

XXII

Once more the distances lie still. Wet trees
are dripping dry. The wind, that shook
the roof and made the chimney howl,
died in the night, and I have breathed
peace all day and listened to my breathing.
To be alone is always new.
Yes, sorting stuff entails juxtaposition,
and juxtaposition calls for skill, an eye
for moments in which light and dark
concuss, so insight can ignite,
and also talent, to choose times of day
when objects are most likely to become
what they resemble, and resist
the pull to readjust to what they are.
Here's to the hills o' the brave and the free!
A hero, James, bites more than he can chew.
Like Milo. And like you and I.
As if conspiratorially,
the sun goes down, and as it does so winks
across the darkening from Kielder Water.

XXIII

Ah! Silly people, how are they deceived!
While wrath abideth, striking sparks
that kindle secretly and don't forgive,
it is impossible but that offences
dividing us, maintaining our division,
shall rise from notions that the world
conceives about us, and cries forth,
that we are dregs, upstarts of the northern parts,
belittling scripture in our pride
and ignorance, who own instead no text
but newly fangled and impious tracts
honouring ourselves, a bloody kennel
infecting innocent and harmless souls,
intent to root out piety and order.
Enough. You find me sleeping on a table
at Martha Simmonds' house. My words
have been mistaken and will misbehave.
A fever grips me, that compounds
both doubt and weakness, and grows more severe
as altercation spreads and poison seeps
into my mind from voices that demand –
in these adulterous and foolish days –
a miracle, to be a sign
to all the world of my immediate sending,
for which they bid me tempt the Lord.
Christ speaks thus, and the Apostles,
but what canst *thou* say? So speaks George.
And so do I, and also this –
is not the Lord's work always overturning,
overturning, overturning?

XXIV

The season tilts. Hawthorn and horse chestnut trees
were showing by the end of March. Frogs and toads
have croaked, and swallows scribble air
in order to remind them where they live.
Next, the ash and sycamore and elm, in bud
together, the cuckoo and the nightingale,
and presently the greening of the oak.
My overturning is of boxes. Clutter
bestrews the floor, awaiting aggregation
according to its provenance or function.
Bookshelves have been commissioned. That's a start.
An anchored bicycle for exercise
will stand so I can view Green Rigg,
where lambs lie in clusters on yon bonny brae,
and cloudscapes, ever changing and unchanging,
speeding up into a wide-screen flicker
which is the twentieth-century middle age
I lived through then, and peer at now,
as in a rear-view mirror, darkly trying
to work out how it thinned so soon
into a blurry memory. And I
shall pay attention, James, while pedalling
in sunlight from the glass front door.

XXV

O England, thou hast never wanted Warnings.
I have stood witness in thy Towns
and Market Streets for most four years.
Is it that your souls have no more value
than make a sport of time? What more,
O England, can be said of you
but thou art fat and full and fit for slaughter?

201

And Martha, could it be that you bewitched me?
I see you sometimes suddenly
through George's eyes, when you approached him, bidding
that he bow down because his heart is rotten,
and singing in his face, inventing words.
I have also known you fall to singing
and the substance, many times repeated,
be always innocency, innocency,
with every repetition meaning less.
That we may bind or loose we have the Word,
the ploughshare forged to till the mind,
that evil would beat into blades.
But be not unadvised or rash
that thou canst bind a brother or a sister –
such an one as hath trespassed against thee –
beneath a greater trespass, giving Satan
advantage that's beyond their strength. For this
the Lord does not delight in, though
you call it just. The time will come
when he that showed no mercy must have judgement
without mercy. And to that end
God has given us forgiveness
that we may walk in, even where
the enemy gains entrance, and men wipe
their mouths and take their fill of mirth.
So Tush, they say, the Lord is gone far off
and seeth not, there is no Revelation.
Martha, your Delftware dish, foremost among
the things I wake to recognise
each morning from unrestful sleep,
reminds us both, in script of cobalt blue,
that 'You and I are Earth'. Have faith. It's true.
But do not hanker for what's better left,
for we are also vessels of the Spirit.

XXVI

Malcolm Mooney is a burly cat. His land
encompasses my garden. He will sleep
beside me on the coldest nights,
and in bed like a person, paws and nose
above the quilt and in the air that turns
our breath to smoke in candlelight.
He is not sentimental. He enjoys
to hunt and kill and disembowel creatures
made smaller and less cunning than himself.
He pays his rent in carcasses.
And I have business with the Wanney Crags
that also needs to be unsentimental:
Aid Crag, an' Luma, an' Hepple Heugh too,
the kindnesses of light on them,
their pitchfork-tossing pines and crouching sheep.

XXVII

Lord mayors of London, Tichborne, Chiverton,
Ireton and Allen, then Sir Robert Browne,
in fear of the Fifth Monarchists –
'King Jesus and their heads upon the gates' –
march their soldiers into our Bull Meeting,
smashing windows, hacking doors and benches,
striking Friends with muskets and the flat of swords,
herding us to prisons rife with pestilence.
In Newgate, Ludgate, Bridewell, and the compters
of Wood Street and The Poultry, day by day,
suffering is our divine communion.
Yet we continue to assemble, bearing
witness equally, not having ministers,
'opposing Government by standing still'
despite the numbers that they apprehend.

Our good Friend Thomas Ellwood was arrested
and sent to Newgate from the Bull and Mouth,
thence, and with two hundred others,
to walk to Bridewell with no guards.
He counselled them, 'we have no stronger keepers
with God's help than our promises'.

XXVIII

The author is dispensable. I crave
no prestige of the individual.
These words alone plod, on a July day,
a quiet zigzag among pines and spruce.
Wind combs the tree-tops. On the forest floor,
all's still, until a sudden shock
emergence on a rocky slope.
Tangling ferns and snatching heather
draw down the breeze head-on. *In faith,*
seek watchful, diligent, and patient meekness.
Cross-country cyclists – angels bright in lycra –
are climbing up Great Wanney Crag,
their glinting bikes like wings across their bodies.

XXIX

Yea, such we have sought long, and what obtained?
I know not, though 'twill make me seek again.
But thou, impatient with prestige,
snug on thy hill, what shalt thou seek?
Hast thou an itch to reach an understanding
with literary theory?
Come down, come down, ye high and lofty one –
magister in artibus, stipendiary
practitioner of adult education –

repent in sackcloath and lie low, and prise
thy time before the door of mercy shuts
forever, and the swallows come
to nest inside the porch and find thee gone,
whilst thou art groping in the dark at noon day
and do not prosper in thy ways,
but stumble in thy fallen wisdom,
as sayeth Deuteronomy and John.
O thou wild and wanton one! Thou ranst too fast
across Northumberland to claim
thy trove of books and solitude – thy gin
at bedtime, *Va pensiero*, and Purcell –
for all there is a Royal Diadem,
as also doth Isaiah speak,
within our uncleane hearts which puts to shame
the vanities that we pursue. But hearken
until such time thine inner eye will open,
then shalt thou know what true Redemption is.

XXX

I treasure your advice. But something's wrong.
Look. The fire-irons fly their flags of shadow
as if they've never been disturbed.
And look. A corridor of light connects
two brightnesses, the window view –
moorland textured like chenille, a strand
of distant cattle – and that square of floor
with mud left by a shoe. The Tilley lamp,
that both illuminates and warms, has flown
from off the mantelpiece. A cupboard door
swings open. I begin to think
a list of absences. What matters is
that someone has been here when I was not.
And Malcolm cannot speak of what he saw.

XXXI

Forget thy sad possessions. In Bristol,
during the Good Friday Blitz, the year thou wert
begat, before thou knew'st of this work,
a length of tram-rail like a thunderbolt
struck St Mary's churchyard from a sky of flame.
It pierced that prayerful tongue of land
as to its hilt. Ezekiel did not
glimpse this. Nearby, it has become October
and deeper yet in civic memory.
We gain the city by the Redcliffe Gate –
from Bedminster into Jerusalem,
as on the first Palm Sunday. We approach,
between the second and the third
hour of the afternoon, by dirty ways
in which the carts and horses and none else
do usually go. Thou may'st object
that God expects no such extremity
but thus we persevere – in rain
so hard as we receive it at our necks
it's venting at our hose and breeches – singing
with such a buzzing and melodious noise
we cannot tell the words of what we sing.
Blessed is he that cometh in the name
across four centuries. My tired horse slithers
on the unevenness of time
and shies at garments, cast into the path
by Martha, Hannah Stranger, and young Dorcas,
who says I raised her from the dead
when she lost sense in gaol in Exeter,
among the beasts there, foaming out their venom.
Hosanna and *Hosanna*, we proceed,
drunk with the indignation of the Lord,
as far as Broad Street, to the White Hart Inn
where the women dry their hair before the fire
and we are seized. Fresh furrows corrugate

the foreheads of the magistrates,
ploughed by the subtlety and reticence
with which I meet their questions. When I do.
Such is the singing – *Holy, Holy, Holy* –
and such the concourse, that examination
as night falls shall not come to much.
Nor shall thy thief. To steal from thee
will bring him little gain but shame. I see
thy door upon the hill remains unlocked.

XXXII

Be valiant, and put on resolution.
The kingdom of the Lord is of a growing
nature. It is like leaven, or like salt,
like morning light that overspreads
to gather mankind to itself. Alas,
as I have said before, I say again,
the spirit of the world seeks to destroy
vessels wherein Truth appeareth, and wherefrom
it shineth forth. Though we are innocent
and simple to the Serpent's subtlety,
yet we are represented as deceivers,
witches, even Jesuits, yea anything
that may be held in perfect detestation,
so that which rules below may keep
its territories in entirity.
On Saturday, which is the Seventh Day,
letters from my pockets are exhibited
with sly solemnity. To wit:
'Everlasting Son of God and Prince of Peace
which no more James shall be but Jesus.'
Yes, I am a Son of God. And one in whom
the everlasting righteousness is wrought.
Such is no blasphemy. Have we not all
one father? So says Malachi.

Have we not all received, moreover,
the Spirit of adoption, heirs henceforth
of God and joint with Christ, as Paul
assures the Romans, thus to be delivered
even from the bondage of corruption?

XXXIII

You have convinced me thus. My task, however,
is vital. I'm Aquarius.
Autumnal air is mild and resonant
as noon turns and stands motionless.
The surface of the spring is oily tea
and breeding, till I shovel mud
to clear the outflow, and the water chuckles
at my reflection, with its own sweat rising,
looming as a silhouette, that's lowering
the jerry-can to heave out with a grunt,
and lug back home across the fell
to drink from, and to wash with, and grow wiser.

XXXIV

Lords, gentlemen, and most respectfully,
we that are your loyal mayor and aldermen –
the council of this city, ministers
and divers chief inhabitants of Bristol –
have too long suffered under much reproach
and ignominy brought about
by increase of a generation rife
among us of seduced and – worse,
and for the Devil's sake – most actively
seducing persons. Such wickedness as theirs
was in our lifetimes formerly unknown,

208

yet we are destitute of legislation
wherewith to punish or restrain
and consequently must stand by, unable
to halt their vile unchristian acts
or put an end to their confused
tumultuous meetings. So it is
that one most eminent, a ringleader
risen tall in open horrid blasphemies,
avows expressly, owned by his followers,
that he is the begotten Son of God.
Since providence has brought extremity
to this degree at such a time
that legislative powers we trust
to moderate the evils of the age
have been convened, we make an application
that straight away your honours shall take up
the reins of government into your hands –
which have too long in this particular
lain loose – to curb henceforth the insolencies
of all ungodly persons and those liberties,
unbridled and licentious, which eclipse
the glory of our Christian profession,
that this reproach – not only of our city
but of the nation and the government –
be rolled away for good by wholesome law.

XXXV

Next to the stove there is a whiff
of Calor gas and, in a cooling saucepan,
a stew of odds and ends of doggerel
that still looks edible. Your namesake, James –
that's Armstrong, of the ballad of the Wannys –
the bard who left it simmering,
is out there somewhere in the snow.
According to the calendar that hangs

209

in gloaming by the kitchen door,
this afternoon is nineteen-eighty-six
and winter has arrived, but he –
with good warm trousers on I trust
beneath his flapping ballad-plaid –
is finding blossoms for his book
in those bleak reaches, that are all too real
despite their name for nowhere hereabouts,
and stumbling where the gorcocks strut
in season among jabbing pines.
When he is here and speaks, his verses soothe
the always present absences
of those – so many nowadays –
that need me to remember them,
and breathe their names, so they can recollect
who they once were and how. More snow
is drifting over Fourlaws Fell. I raise
a glass to him, then pour myself another.

XXXVI

Today is also sixteen-fifty-six,
and we are brought to London, singing through
the most part of the towns to admiration,
that is to say astonishment,
and lodged here with the messenger
from Bristol, by the marketplace
at Westminster, and hailed to Parliament
where Thomas Bampfield, and his half-a-hundred
committee-men – all fearing God
and being also of good conversation –
are waiting to examine us,
the better to discover blasphemy
and misdemeanor, and the proof thereof.
Faithful to the end of all injustice,
so shall we ever seek that which is perfect –

that Kingdom never to be done away.
Again, and wearily, I must explain
that it had pleased the Lord to raise me up
not as I am, a creature, but a sign
to point the coming of the righteous one,
and that I am commanded by the Lord
to suffer thus, and do abhor that honour
due to God should come to me. Yet they insist
that I assumed the gestures and the words,
the incommunicable attributes
and titles of our Saviour,
together with His miracles. *Alas,*
let none deceive, whatever they imagine.
We are born through sorrow and are slain with ease,
so watch and wait, and in the Light stand ready.

XXXVII

So. They heard me out, and what they heard they deemed
such as ungodded God. My punishment
it was proposed be death. The noes, however,
stood ninety-six, while yeas stood eighty-two.
So passed the negative. And of that mercy,
came first of all the pillory, and then
they whipped me tethered to a cart, the lash
comprising seven knotted cords,
applied upon each crossing of a sewer,
from Palace Yard to Old Exchange, which made
fifteen score and ten. But some that counted
pronounced this short, because the hangman missed
his footing, cutting his own hand.
Those that scrutinised me at the end confirmed
that no space broader than a fingernail
remained, according to their best discernment,
between my shoulders and my waist
free from blood and stripes, and that the horses

the bailiffs rode had trod me down so hard
their shoes were printed on my feet.
My hands were bloody also, and much swollen.
In such condition, wretched to the danger
even of my life, I was allowed to rest
nine days, till foolish Christ-tide had begun,
then sent from Newgate in a coach
to the Black Boy inn whence, fenced with halberds,
to the pillory again where Robert Rich –
esteemed the perfect maniac,
though verily religious – preached, while Martha,
Hannah Stranger and young Dorcas Erbury,
disposed themselves as the three Marys did
upon Golgotha. There I strained and stretched,
from noon until the hour of two,
then was unclamped. Next, with my neck
bound to the post, the executioner
pulled down a cap to cover up my eyes
and bade me to put out my tongue. That done,
he bored it through with an hot iron
about the bigness of a quill,
and then, by order of the sheriff, held
it there for some short space, for all beholders
to see and thus bear witness to.
Then, having drawn it out, and pulling off
my cap, did put a handkerchief
across my eyes, his left hand to the back
part of my head to grip, and took
a second iron that had the letter B
hot from his brazier and set
it to my forehead, so it smoaked and hissed
while signifying blasphemy,
and all the time the people, both
before me and behind me and beside,
stood there bareheaded, as with one consent,
while not a thing at all was thrown
and few reviled. Robert Rich then held my hand

to help me down, and kissed the fire
out from my wound. All day they tried
to silence him. Nor have his like
been quiet since. At last unbound, I took
the man that muted and disfigured me
into my arms, embracing him,
as if to comprehend what had been done.

XXXVIII

Friend, sunlight of four centuries
shines in between me and your suffering.
And beasten have been getting in the garden
on rubble where the wall is down.
They eat all they can see. I must
attend to that. *O Wannys, wild Wannys!*
The scene it is grand! Who daubed stone
around a long-gone kitchen range
with gluey black, and then a coat of cream,
and liked the look? I'm tapping at a riffler,
combing a texture, golden-brown
on chimney-back, on side-slabs, and the lintel
that stand in dust and will not move. Tap tap.
A heart-beat in a cold stone house. A hearth
for my wood-burning stove. Next on the list:
re-point the gable, where the wet west wind
blows in above the window with the view
as far as Roxburghshire. Up here,
there's always work for me to do. And Malcolm
to keep an eye on how I'm getting on.

XXXIX

Please listen. I must tell thee, through the light,
next how I was sent again to Bristol,
in order that my sentence be completed.
And how, from Lawford's Gate to Redcliffe Gate,
I rode a bareridged horse, to face the tail,
and then to Thomas Street, there stripped and made
fast to a cart once more, and from the market
whipped to Bridge Foot, whipped, and Bridge End, whipped,
and at the High Street and the Tolzey, whipped,
then Broad Street, whipped, and at the Taylor's Hall
released. One Jones, a coppersmith esteemed
an ugly Quaker, was for that day suffered,
out of clemency and to the credit
of the magistracy of that city,
to pull back at the beadle's arm when striking.
And all the while I passed along
Robert Rich rode with his meer-maid's head –
such was his length of hair – aloft before me
chanting *Holy, Holy, Holy.*

XL

O England, thou art making thyself drunken
with Blood that is the Blood of Innocence,
which Blood it is that crieth loud
into the ears of God. And now the time
is come that nothing satisfies but Blood.
Yea, he will give thee Blood to drink, and Blood
above thy Horse's bridle, Blood to thy throat.
Thou light, thou vain, that lift thy heel
to kick against the Lord thy God, his sword
now drawn against thee will be sheathed,
O England, in thy bowels. Blood shalt thou weep
for slackness of desire for thy salvation.

XLI

At last to Bridewell, sickening
and from society restrained, to labour
till, a year before I quit this earthen life
to be where conversation is in Heaven –
and Cromwell having left behind confusion –
all Quakers were by Parliament released.
My cell had two doors and three locks.
I did not eat unless I worked the hemp:
nine pence for five and twenty pounds.
Such was I thought the nadir of my fortunes.
Anne was allowed to see me. After that
the boards beneath my feet were levered up
to look for pen and ink, for even then
they feared my words. The cough increased upon me
which has afflicted me since soldiering
but then they designated Mistress Pollard,
that was an ancient widow, as my keeper
and something of my strength returned. *Behold,*
behold, ye poor despisèd ones,
how holy men of God travail in sorrow
to bring forth that which He begets
contrary to the world. And so did I,
the doubter always plucking at my sleeve,
and not a jot of it my own conceiving.
Yet still the Lord upheld me. Although Satan
had power to winnow me as wheat,
my life was hid with Him. Amen.

XLII

The generator handle's lost its grip,
and will not crank that beast into the roar
that shakes the light awake, and powers the pump.
I lack your zeal, James. But I pay attention.
My gostly fader, to God first, then to you
I me confesse. My father put on khaki
and went, like you, to war. Like you, he failed
to live long after he returned. I think
your voices are alike. I don't remember.
But evening draws the three of us together
where there's a log fire, a new Tilley lamp –
health, peace and plenty, for ever and aye,
on the wild hills o' Wannys far, far away –
and time to know how small the time we share,
but then how great the sadness and delight,
and always gin and water from the spring
that's rich in iron, which is beneficial,
or from the gutter, gargling distances.
Fix thine eye upon the mark, my friend. Pass on.
Here's to the future. I look back from there.

XLIII

The road is featureless, and fields are slick
beneath autumnal rain. Blackberries shrivel
along hedgerows. Steeplehouses
point from the levels to a flat grey sky.
A Friend at Hertford, when I stopped there, came
upon me by the highway. He perceived
my awful weighty state of mind,
and begged to take me back with him to rest.
But I refused. Such little strength I have
must push one foot before the next for home,

my wife, my fields, through shrinking days,
to Huntingdonshire, and then across the town
where I am seen to pass close by
the Falcon Inn, where Cromwell kept
his table. I am recognised
as one not owning anything, a soul
redeemed from earth, a stranger on it, seeking
a better dwelling and inheritance.
Go, sayeth George. Now over fen-land north,
the wind lamenting, as it seems, the droves
still featureless, except for pools
of standing water, till at last:
Jesus, he stinks! Get hold of him I dare you!
Do they call you Jesus? That your name? Jesus?
One punches me. Another shoves.
Tie his hands and legs! Get hopping, Jesus man!
You got no home to go to? God you stink.
In England I was four and forty years
to reach this mire, this night, thrown down
within sight of a place named Holme, where Friends
would harbour me. Instead, a countryman
a bit like you, his mind upon the hearth-glow
he is belatedly returning to
in these parts, stumbles on me, bound
and robbed of what I know not. I have nothing.

Vade Mecum

Forget the page you're reading. Here's another
I need to introduce you to. Begin
by noticing the colour. It's off-white.

Off-brown. Off-orange at the edges. Light
for donkeys' years has crept and made it darken,
even on the shelf. It's pulp. Print, front to back,

shows faintly from the other side, in spaces
between the paragraphs. Breathe in and savour
the fragrance of the centre crease,

which is old sawmill dust, as thick as planks.
Let words act up. Endure obscure quotations,
chases in Arras, dreams in a career,

articulacy in vast void that bounds
all thought, and all endeavour. Here
is where we start. A lodging house in ———,

a door that has been locked for days,
a man, dead in his chair when we break in,
and deep gloom, thicker than before the dawn

on mountain top, by lonely shore or hanger.
His face has set fast in the look
that has seen nothing you and I would see.

I hope we never will. I love this book.

Graduands

He sits and smiles, his back towards the bureau,
which is an arm's length from the hearth –
a fireplace, framing a bouquet
of dried flowers, grasses, twigs and teasels.

We sense, perhaps, the end of youth. The décor
ensures that untaught glances are directed
straight to good taste. There's a cow-hide carpet
on gleaming pine. His books form ranks

by size and shape and not by theme or author.
We're here to say that we have him to credit
for our success. Exaggeration sizzles
but lacks the warmth to thaw the conversation.

He knew a famous novelist. A picture,
picked up before the artist was renowned,
is enigmatic on the wall. Politics
is out of bounds. His family. The war.

The challenge for the Beast, he quotes,
is Patience. That for Beauty is Perception.
He is an educator to his boots.
Well then. Goodbye. He has the Evening News

unopened. In its designated nook
the television set stands blankly by.
Tonight, however, is the time for truth.
And the bureau. Its polished oak

reflects the bright glow of the Anglepoise.
He drops the lid and chooses for perusal
a journal, written in a schoolboy cypher,
which proves beyond all doubt what we suspected.

The Scare

The pressure's off. We are as safe as houses,
at least for now. But come with me,
let's do some peeping-in through half-drawn curtains.
Behold, well-plenished dinner-party guests
linger at table, ready to withdraw.
And they are pensive. They have heard the news.
Science has identified the microbe
that's causing outbreaks of imagination
across the world. Its source could be
an inner eye, an inmost ear,
some obscure extra organ of perception.
But they suspect it's spread by us. Take care.
Stay well-informed. It is against
such windows that we're wise to press our noses.

À Côté de la Sorgues

Petrarch, I've dreamed up a maxim for you
a propos of nothing. *Mais* please excuse
such importunity. It's hardly news
that I have yet to climb *my* Mont Ventoux.
It harks back to a long lunch long ago
in a basement café – level with the shoes
of passers-by – in Fontaine de Vaucluse.
The challenge: create an aphorism. Now.
No chance. But later on I tried again.
Nothing comes to hand by accident makes sense.
In fact it's downright clever, if I'm honest.
Rien se produit par hasard à la main.
You'd know that, father of the Renaissance.
Laureate and lover. Fixer. Alpinist.

Iron Railings

I'm getting nowhere and I'm out of breath.
Re-hear-sal stupid, re-hear-sal stupid:
the secret, so the pigeons say,
is practice, practice, then, through repetition,
wing-purchase on the sunlit air, redemption
in distant neighbourhoods, and swoops of joy.
Alas for bipedality.
I'm of the earth. I'm clinging on
to limitation like grim death.
And iron railings, on a cold wet day.

MCMLVI

The desk clerk's dressed in black.
Heartbreak Hotel

'Of metamorphosis, let us assume' –
he raps a knuckle on the board –
'that shapes exist or pre-exist
already, waiting to engage with substance
and blossom in the flowerbed of form.
Tomorrow we'll discuss the imago.'
On playing fields beyond the classroom window,
a mower swerves behind a tractor
in silent distance and a shower of grass.
He has unfurled a visual aid. He prods
its crackled surface with a thin sharp pointer.

What it reveals we can't quite see.
Not Elvis, that's for sure. There goes the bell.
He twirls. His gown is grey with chalk. He is
a chalky butterfly. I'll have you know,
it is that kind of school. 'As you depart,
consider. The relative longevity
of memories of days like these, says Proust,
together with poetical –
if one dare use the term – associations,
will transcend that of everything the heart
may subsequently suffer. Class dismissed.'

The Promenade

I know. You got enough of wind and rain
at war-time bus stops at your mother's knee.
Then, in the dull slog of your prime, more rain.
Now you're old and cold, and still the weather's thrawn
and in the mood to throw a drench
right through you as you trudge beside the sea.

Buck up. The foreshore with its links and lawns
is always thirsty. Don't complain.
It puts off visitors. Look, at a pinch
come under my umbrella and keep dry.
If it blows inside-out, we'll start again.
When worse descends to worst, you are still me.

The Lucky Ones

We don't wish to upset you. Even so,
since you're repolishing your aspirations,
we need to state the obvious.

That's what we're for. We speak to you
in words you almost think, and thus
the whispering you almost hear continues.

You're scared to listen. That amuses us.
It's as you say. We are the lucky ones.
You have your share of dying still to do.

Taliesin

The key won't turn because the door's not locked,
as if you thought you'd not be gone for long
then disappeared for sixty years.
Someone has been and emptied out the place
leaving a cold, thin, hippie, joss-stick smell.
But Robert Graves is where he often was,
propped open on the mantelpiece,
and here's that riddle from the *Book of Hengest*,
in English from the ancient Welsh,
marked by a faded bus ticket to Crumpsall.

A dog barks somewhere, answered by a yell
half-human in the echoes of the street.
And now you listen to the empty grate.
The fire is dead. So are your words, it whispers,
unless you're mad and dream, like Taliesin
wily in his many guises,
that you'll become the grain that's pecked
up by Cerridwen and reborn in song
to carry home the yearned-for, outright prizes
while rivals squawk in hen-yard dust.

The Floor Above

I wake from an involuntary prayer
to hear my voice complain that God is not –
and never was – a Gentleman
who takes my interests to heart
eternally. That's immature.
Just then a door slams on the floor above,
and there's religious ruckus on the landing
outside the brain I'm thinking in.
So off I go to see what that's about.
When I come back no doubt I'll pray again.
Perhaps I'll find that, while we've breath to spare
to rigmarole our rigmaroles,
a certain silliness may prove
His kindest ordinance for saving souls.

Night Wanderers

I'm still not sure of your identity,
despite those reminiscences –
that cliff path after evening rain
we dared not tread for crunching snails. That night
we bathed beneath an old town bridge. *En France*.
When we were young. Hello again.
You say my state of mind is so well lit
that mischief has succumbed to probity
and made me the epitome
of dullness fused with common sense.
D'accord. Let's do some more noctivagance.
When it gets dark we'll hit the street
and see how many nightmares sit
on bedroom windowsills. We'll let them in.

Ex Sublimis

> Then will I sprinkle clean water upon you,
> and you shall be clean ... and from all
> your idols will I cleanse you.
>
> EZEKIEL 36: 25

As merit, luck, or privilege affords,
wisdom trickles down here in this library
and learning for the sake of it evolves
where gothic glass yields mellow light
and scholars in black gowns climb towering stacks
like bats, the higher the more erudite,
on frail ladders or, with trembling bravery,
unaided, clinging to the slithery books
by toes and fingertips. Alas, sheer fright
grips them sometimes and they sprinkle –
apologies, Ezekiel,
I didn't want to say they piss themselves –
but we can live with that. They risk their necks
to cleanse the idols of the day
from tender minds below. The benefit
drums down upon our tasselled mortarboards.

Icarus

How right they always were, the old schoolmasters,
to say we teach till faces blur.
Some duty, what it was I don't remember,
placed me in a classroom on that Saturday
and at a window, where I leaned
as teams below ran out into September
sunshine and invigorating air. The turf
was not so smooth, the matched fifteens so vivid,
as I recall them now. Shadows extend.
The flags hang limp and yet the ball's alive.
There's a kerfuffle, followed by hiatus.
The game's been halted. There's a player down.
Now someone grabs to lift him. Muddy shirts
trudge back towards the changing room.
But he stays where he lies. His limbs have jammed.
I taught him. I forget his name.
He lived to see his parents growing old,
and when the right day came he rolled
his wheelchair to their garden pond
and somehow tipped it, so he slid
face first. There's no one there to watch, or snatch,
and there's no splash, and no forsaken cry.
But fifty years ago I start to worry
to see how late into the afternoon
the ambulance stands parked out on the pitch.

The Doorstop

Marilyn, after fourteen takes, your silly
frock above the subway grate, on Lexington
and Fifty-second, billows up,
an opening flower you clutch at modestly
to publicise *The Seven Year Itch*.
And ooh, the breeze is warm, you say. And ooh.

The flower is you. I know because I own –
and this would make you laugh – that smile,
that instant, cast into an iron doorstop
and heavy in my hands. The irony.
A naughty glimpse could be a lethal weapon
like chloral hydrate or like Nembutal.

I'll leave it on the mat to serve its purpose.
The love and rage of Joe DiMaggio,
and roses on your grave for twenty years,
were what they were. But art endures.
Light flicks through darkness as I watch
your half-shy pose of impudence. Your beauty.

Vale Royal

We can see you, leaning on a gate. Hello.
Your shadow is now creeping back
to touch the fringes of the copse
you have been strolling through. Behold
the Vale Royal of England or some other
prospect before you, and a country seat
you unexpectedly inherited.

It seems congratulations are in order.
You have obtained a good degree,
and very soon we hear you will be married.
Why not indulge yourself and wear
the day as if it were your Barbour jacket?
High time for home. Outside the door
you stop to fumble with the key.

Air shivers and a bird's nest drops
to land between your feet, light, dry, and empty.
You pick it up to scrutinise. We're worried.
Toss the thing away. Forget it.
Remain that lucky and resourceful fellow
who lacks for nothing here below,
nor wants that nothing to be emblematic.

Klutvang

The glow, glimpsed intermittently, is bright,
but still too spooky to permit
relaxed absorption in anticipation.
We shall be hopeful and not make a fuss.
The source from which originality
must spring is nature, says John Constable.
And he should know. He learned to look.

And yet his aim was always artifice.
Mine too. We have arrived. My first impression
requires a word from that unwritten tongue –
beguiling but resistant to translation –
which is the language of the song
God is crooning *sotto voce* –
klutvang, which means *strange* but also *homely*.

The staff pick up our luggage. Brisk and helpful,
discreet but cheerful, they are not put out
one bit by our abrupt and late arrival.
They call to mind friends loved and gone
but back again, by years forsook.
They learn our habits. They have wings of light.
And nature formed them to rejoice in us.

Gestalt

It's psychological. A sleepy cat
will always see a small thing move.

Likewise, although the world is stacked
with evidence that it should not be loved,

unfinished beauty is a fact
that keeps love wakeful till a pounce completes it.

Neck Verse

Itch leads to scratch, when all is said and done,
that's why you had your collar felt,
and 'done' and 'said' got you banged up. Your guilt
pervades the cell. Your crimes include
clever but unnecessary poetry,
trimmed with reach-me-down ideas
selected to amuse a coterie
applauding at the edge of mind-shot, plus
lack of ambition, bigged-up as a virtue,
and an annoying smirk. Sign this confession –
don't try to forge my signature –
then hand it over in the light of dawn
when they unbolt the door and shout your number.
Enjoy your breakfast, Maestro. I'll be gone.

The Kite

The string breaks and the kite drifts loose –
a bright but shifty metaphor –
aloft in dust-shine from the court-room windows.
It flutters this way, that way down
to rest beside the tight shoes of the judge.
You are the judge. So clear my name.
Get justice done. Turn back the clock
and start my life afresh, this time for fun.

What's more fun than a *fête champêtre*?
Let's have some jugglers and stilt-walkers, dressed
as flamingoes and clowns, face-painters,
Punch and Judy shows, a jazz band, rock bands,
and a string quartet. There should be waiters,
chefs in their chef's hats, barbecues,
seafood bars, oysters, a spit-roast with crackling,
and *crêpes* and fruits, sufficiencies of booze.

But the kite has caught the breeze out through the door
and got snagged in a tree of blame
by prickly twigs of evidence.
I'm mind-cuffed to my conscience in the dock
and nothing I can say will make it budge.
Chuck law at it. Proclaim my innocence.
When it's free, I'm free. And the party's on.
The future's here. Your invitation stands.

The Refugee

(after a poem by Mary Anne Perkins)

Your words are apt. You're right. A fledgling tumble
allows no fear to grow. Air gave his skin
all he was due of rushed maternal kisses
bestowed before brief absences.
I try to guess what might be seen
and moved towards within his moment's brightness.

What purpose there? What pang of joy
taught him to recognise – your words recur –
the shortest way beyond experience?
He had no chance or need to dream
a hard new language. This one. Or
to unremember words his first thoughts were.

He's closed his eyes and neither thinks nor listens.
Let's leave him. We must not conspire
along with history to make him seem
more like an emblem than a boy
who fled so far from home to fall
and teach us what our lives and deaths resemble.

On 18 August 2021, the five-year-old son of refugees forced to flee from
Afghanistan fell to his death from a high hotel window.

Hemistich

How soon it's late December. Shadows race
full tilt to dim the shrubbery,
and lavender grows dark in died-back clumps
outside my window, on the balcony
in cold damp heavy pots. The problem is,
years' endings call for a reprise
of what has been too often said.
Too bad. I'll speak out once more to deny
the insignificance of dwindling days
and readily turn down the lamps
on half a line of verse, a thought, a place.
It is the season to put hopes to bed.

An Invitation

My journey will of course entail enquiries
in which you could assist, to find
answers that refresh the questions
concerning who we are and where, and how
might Why be circumvented. Please
come with me for a little way. The stars,
those memories and glittering reminders,
that rose when I set out, descend.
The long road urges. Resonance
is fading from the echoes. We should go.

The Goodbye Note

I Samuel 25: 20, 31, 34

I peer up close at texture, form and colour,
as I have done since infancy
and hope for actuality,
real stuff I can rely upon
not suddenly to change, but to retain
its quiddity, and stay where it is put.

Yet I enjoy quotation and pretence,
the drawing-room on stage, the snobbery,
those radiant mornings just beyond the door
into the gloomy wings. *Come on,*
the actor calls, *come on, the taxi's here!*
The backdrop trembles. It is really not.

If it were, then I would have it take me
down by the covert of the hill
into a summer of imagination,
and leave this goodbye note, already written,
which offers no offence of heart to any
that piss against the wall. Or any lady.

Shadowed Water

You have seen nothing yet. The octopus
at the aquarium, that changes colour
as it examines you, the squid
next tank along, that has enough IQ
to do Sudoku, but does not, the trees
outside the window, all insist
that everything that is exists in one
eternal *jeu d'esprit* that makes things new
and will do, even when your life has slid
away into a patch of shadowed water,
disturbing fronds behind the glass
but out of sight beyond your own reflection.

My Mephistopheles

He's quite straightforward when he offers me
the opportunity to realise
what I most want, and puts a price on it.
I'm glad of that. Need calls for clarity.
And I am drawn to the lucidity
which is essential to his name and nature.
Our conversations dart like quick manoeuvres
amid fast traffic on a busy road,
and he and I above it in the air,
then there's a sudden stop, a staircase up,
at nightfall to a medieval attic
among the spires of somewhere else,
a pentagram chalked on a dusty floor.
His presence fills the gloom, his eyes become
scintillas of reflected candle-glow.
There is a burning smell. My senses blur
in an equivalence of opposites,
and in a mist of greed that hides
his actuality. I hesitate.
Then I step through a mirror and shake hands
with smoke. He is informal and engaging.

I can't help smiling when he's making light
of my domestic obligations.
He's up to mischief though. He has a story
he tells as if to entertain the children,
about a spider and a fly.
It frightens them. It frightens *me*. His use
of make-up is for sure a touch eccentric –
those hints of horns and poodle ears –
but all in character and comical.
His manners are impeccable.
He knows the people people know, and he
is ready with a small *cadeau*

whenever he appears. He'll not
outstay his welcome, or delay
before he sends a scorch-marked note of thanks.
His tailoring conceals his tail.
Its spear-like point, I'm fairly sure,
is tucked into his sock. He's erudite,
wide-ranging and alert in talk, and even
a little snobbish in a kindly way,
which makes for ease and confidence.

He's keen to tell me how alike we are,
and so attentive that I'm reassured –
although I lack both wealth and influence
and am not aspirational –
that I exist in some enduring sense
and what I might pluck up the nerve to wish
could here and now and readily be granted.
Despite all this, of course, and while
it's him I recognise behind the faces
of those I am most eager to impress,
we are not friends. He is a fiend.
It's evident that, if his propositions
reveal a vision of my world made perfect,
they pertain only to emergencies
in which the soul, befuddled by the body,
is comatose and easy prey.
Their plausibility and glitter pall.
Get him behind me and back home to hell.
There's no damn way we'll reach an understanding.
But he knows where I live. We'll stay in touch.
It does me good to meet a gentleman.

NOTES

The story of the long pack appears in *The Ettrick Shepherd's Tales*, and also in Elizabeth Gaskell's *Cranford*. It is well known in the village of Bellingham, in Northumberland, where the occupant of the pack is buried in the churchyard. My poem adds details of his earlier life, as a member of a community of Ranters, to material provided by James Hogg, together with an account of some episodes in the lives of two late-twentieth-century lovers who are troubled by this desperado's restless and rather domineering spirit. The haunter's aim is to be reborn and recognised. Meanwhile he describes their experiences as well as his own, offers advice and comment, and appears sometimes in foliage, like the Green Man. The narrator also refers, perhaps unwisely, to links between participants in the 1715 Jacobite uprising in Northumberland and the activities of the mysterious Prieuré de Sion, described by Michael Baigent, Richard Leigh, and Henry Lincoln in *The Holy Blood and the Holy Grail*. The voice of Richard Last, which dominates the chorus, is adapted from the writings of the real-life Ranter Abiezer Coppe. The chorus also includes quotations from Sir George Etherege, Robert Herrick, Samuel Johnson, Andrew Marvell, the anonymous author of 'Hexham Wood', and Wilfrid Gibson, whose poem 'The Unseen Rider' also mentions Heatherbell and the tragic wedding. Apart from a visit to the Coromandel coast, and to the unusual church at Hartburn, the events of the poem all take place in the North Tyne valley and Redesdale. The ruins of The Orchard can still be visited.

JIGGER NODS (75-96)

Iphicles was the son of Amphitrion and his wife Alcmene, but his brother Hercules was the son of Zeus, who had disguised himself as Amphitrion. The relationship of Henry Jigger to his brother, the popular GP, corresponds to that between Hercules and Iphicles, though in this case Zeus had disguised himself as the vicar. As a schoolmaster, somewhere in the northern part of England in the middle of the last century, Jigger likes to dwell, in a muddled sort of way, on the story of the occupation of Albion by the Trojan Brutus, in which Hercules played a part. There is of course no excuse for his disreputable views, moral cowardice and heavy drinking, or for his addiction to Latin tags. Quotations throughout the poem are taken or adapted from *Albion's England* by William Warner, of which C.S. Lewis wrote: 'The good things are as far divided as the suns in space.' The Latin tags may be found underlined in the section headed 'Words and Phrases in More or Less Current Use from Latin, Greek, and Modern Foreign Languages' in Jigger's copy of *Chambers's Twentieth Century Dictionary*, 1939 edition, and, for convenience, below. The exception, *Non Nisi Malis Terrori*, remains the motto of the school that employed him.

Jigger's Latin tags: Aut insanit homo aut versus facit (either the man is mad or making verses); Bis pueri senes (old men are twice boys); Claviger (club-bearer or key-bearer, an epithet of Hercules); Dum vivimus vivamus (while we live, let us live); Eheu fugaces... labuntur anni (alas, the fleeting years slip away); Ex pede Herculem (we recognise Hercules by his foot); Fuimus Troes (we were once Trojans); Necessitas non habet legem (necessity has or knows no law); Obscurum per obscurius (explaining the obscure by means of the more obscure); O zonam perdidit (he has lost his purse, he is in needy circumstances).

FOLLY WOOD (105-15)

George Ripley, who died in 1490, was an important English alchemist. The subtitles of the thirteen sections of the poem are the names of the Twelve Gates, or stages in the alchemical process, as set out in his *Compound of Alchymy*, plus the recapitulation. They are of course in a different order.

Unity in the Englischer Garten (121): Unity Valkyrie Mitford, who liked to call the Nazi stormtroopers 'dear storms', was brought up at Swinbrook in Oxfordshire. She shot herself in the Englischer Garten in Munich in September 1939, shortly after her 25th birthday. She survived to die in Scotland in 1948.

BOBBY BENDICK'S RIDE (123-30)

The Reverend Robert Bendick and the ballad 'Bobby Bendick's Ride', together with other members of the curious and unlucky Bendick family, are mentioned in a story by Sean O'Brien. The ballad is otherwise hitherto unknown. I like to think I heard it twenty or thirty years ago in the Gun Inn in Ridsdale, on the evening of Bellingham Show, but that is impossible, because I wrote it. It appears that Bendick studied in France rather than at Oxford or Cambridge, perhaps to save money or to distance himself from scandal. What is known about his family would suggest the latter. His ordination would have taken place during the time of the Commonwealth, though no record of it has been found, and though his activities at and around the Norman church of St Cuthbert at Corsenside cannot be dated with certainty they clearly took place during the long reign of the 'sordid and scandalous' John Graham, who was the curate there from 1617 to 1682, and, we must assume, with his connivance. Bendick was evidently familiar with Pau and the neighbouring town of Lescar, where the mosaic of the crippled huntsman can be seen in the church of Notre-Dame beside the tombs of some of the kings of Navarre. The Musée des Beaux Arts in Pau houses more paintings on the theme of Tobias and the Angel – alias Azariah – than a visitor might expect, no doubt reflecting the interests of a former benefactor. The city is also proud to be the birthplace of Henry IV of France, whose cradle was a turtle shell, and of Jean-Baptiste Bernadotte, the 'sergeant with beautiful legs', who became King of Sweden. A later member of the English colony in Pau was Major C.W. Mercer, who wrote as Dornford Yates. The genial voice of his creation Bertram 'Berry' Pleydell echoes here and there in the poem. I am indebted to an article by Helen Grant, published in *The Ghosts and Scholars M.R. James Newsletter*, for the information that nine crocodiles are dedicated ancient monuments in France. According to J.C. Cooper and other authorities, the crocodile symbolises duplicity and viciousness but is also considered to be a guardian of knowledge. The jaws of the crocodile represent hell. Wanney Byre is a fissure in the face of Great Wanney Crag. 'Cuddy's kirk' has been repaired since Bendick's time, and is used for occasional services. I have been unable to corroborate a report that children in that secretive corner of Northumberland used to be warned to stay away from Ingram Pool after dark for fear of meeting 'Black Bobby'. There are after all less fanciful reasons to avoid deep water at night.

The Comfort Service (142): In 1926 the photographer Don Gillum took publicity shots of a very uneasy Greta Garbo posing with MGM's mascot, Leo the Lion. The lion belonged to Randall Jarrell's aunt.

A Helpmeet for Protestant Mystics (144): In 'The Protestant Mystics', W.H. Auden asserts that there are four sorts of mystical vision: that of God, that of Agape, that of Eros, and that of Dame Kind. The essay doesn't mention a helpmeet.

The Better Place (145): In a letter to Benjamin Bailey, written in November 1817, Keats tells his friend that 'we shall enjoy ourselves here after (sic) by having what we called happiness on Earth repeated in a finer tone… Adam's dream will do here…'. Elsewhere he recommends 'ardent listlessness' and 'fine suddenness' as good states of mind for poetry. Adam's dream is described in Book VIII of *Paradise Lost*.

Landscape with Psyche (149-55): Paul Valéry also used the quotation from *Psyché*, by Pierre Corneille, as the epigraph of *La Jeune Parque*, translated here by Alistair Elliot. The painting in my poem is *Landscape with Psyche outside the Palace of Cupid*, 1664, by Claude Lorraine, in the National Gallery, London. Here and there I have borrowed phrases from the story of Cupid and Psyche, from *The Golden Ass* by Apuleius, as retold by Thomas Bulfinch and Walter Pater in 1855 and 1885.

Virgil (160): This poem was written in June 2016, after a referendum about Britain's membership of the European Union. According to Erwin Panofsky and others, Virgil invented evening. Oscar Wilde mentions 'milk-white peacocks', quoting from Tennyson's poem 'Now Sleeps the Crimson Petal', in his essay 'The Decay of Lying', 1891, in which he similarly claims that poets gave us the language of twilight.

Ladderedge and Cotislea (163-72): The poem revisits memories from between my war-time early childhood and my father's death in 1953. I was born at Ladderedge, near Leek, in Staffordshire. Cotislea is the name of a house my family lived in later, in Poynton, in Cheshire.

The Gypsy Fiddle (174): I am indebted to *A Classical Dictionary of the Vulgar Tongue* by Francis Grose, originally published in 1785.

My Mother at Erbistock (177): There is an echo here of Charles Kingsley's poem 'The Sands of Dee'. Erbistock is on that river.

Nayler (181-217):
    I 'An' woo' is from 'Wild Hills o' Wannys', 1879, by James Armstrong.
    II 'Apocatastesis' suggests the restoration of prelapsarian innocence. The Greek word 'apokatastesis' occurs once in the New Testament, where it is rendered as 'restitution of all things' in the King James version. See Acts 3: 19-21.

III 'On the wild hills' and 'my gostly fader' are from 'Wild Hills o' Wannys' and 'My Gostly Fader', an early 15th-century rondel attributed to Charles d'Orléans, set to music by Peter Warlock in 1918.

V See Ezekiel 1: 12

VI 'An' listen' is from 'Wild Hills o' Wannys'.

VII George Fox, 1624-1691. 'High notionist' is from James Nayler. Many early Quakers had a deep-rooted mistrust of 'high and lofty' things, particularly intellectual and social aspirations.

XII Yevgeny Yevtushenko, 1933-2017, from *Zima Junction*.

XIII See John 20: 19-26.

XVIII In 'Postuma Christiana', 1712, William Crouch wrote: 'Some part of an Ancient Great House or Building within Aldersgate was taken for a Meeting place the other part of it with a Yard being made a Public for Carriers and Travellers which having for a sign the Bull and Mouth occasioned the meeting to be held there to be known and distinguished by the Name of Bull and Mouth or Bull Meeting.' Quaker meetings took place there from 1655 until the building was destroyed in the Great Fire of 1666.

XIX 'The dark ravens' is from 'Wild Hills o' Wannys'.

XX These sites are in the vicinity of the Barbican. 'I stole a cosse' is from 'My Gostly Fader'.

XXI Nayler was evidently allowed some freedom during his time in Exeter, since he met Fox outside the prison at least twice. Timepiece is on the site of the former gaol. 'Half-decent' is from the nightclub's own publicity.

XXII 'Here's to the hills' is from 'Wild Hills o' Wannys'.

XXIV The list of seasonal changes is adapted from Robert Marsham, writing in 1755. 'Where lambs lie' is from 'Wild Hills o' Wannys'.

XXV 'Bind or loose' is from Matthew 16: 18-19. Nayler writes: 'You may bind or loose here on earth who have the word'. The dish is in the Museum of London.

XXVI 'Aid Crag' is from 'Wild Hills o' Wannys'.

XXIX See Deuteronomy 28: 29, and John 11: 9-10.

XXXI The embedded tram-rail is still in place in St Mary's church-yard in Bristol. See Ezekiel 1: 12.

XXXII See Malachi 2: 10, and Romans 8: 16-21.

XXXIV Between the First Protectorate Parliament and the Second, inaugurated on 17 September 1656, the country had endured nearly two years of thinly disguised military rule.

XXXVI Thomas Bampfield, MP for Exeter, was appointed chair of the committee to examine Nayler. At that time members of parliament were required to be 'persons of known integrity, fearing God, and of good conversation'.

XXXVII Robert Rich was one of Nayler's most faithful supporters. He was a regular presence at the doors of parliament during his trial and sentencing, distributing letters and papers on his behalf and rebuking members.

XXXVIII 'O Wannys' is from 'Wild Hills o' Wannys'.

XLII 'My gostly fader' and 'health, peace and plenty' are from 'My Gostly Fader' and 'Wild Hills o' Wannys'.

XLIII The voices of Nayler's assailants are adapted from Dorothy Nimmo, *A Testimony to the Grace of God in the Life of James Nayler, 1618-1660* (1993).

All other borrowings and quotations, including those in italics, are from James Nayler and Martha Simmonds.

James Nayler was born into a farming family near Wakefield in 1618. He joined the Parliamentary army in 1643 and took part in the Battle of Dunbar. He left the army due to ill-health in 1651, by which time he was quartermaster in General John Lambert's regiment of horse, and known as a gifted extempore preacher. He was well-thought-of, to the extent that Lambert would later say 'we parted with him with great regret'. After returning to farming, he joined an Independent congregation at St Mary Woodkirk, and met George Fox in 1652.

A revelation while ploughing at 'barley seed time', when he heard 'the voice of that God which I had professed as a child but had never known', moved him to set out as one of the travelling Quaker evangelists who became known as the Valiant Sixty. He and Fox were welcomed by Margaret Fell at Swarthmoor Hall in Cumbria, who persuaded her husband, Judge Thomas Fell, to extend his protection to persecuted Quakers.

Apart from a term in prison in Appleby, Nayler preached extensively in northern England during 1653 and 1654. By June 1655 he was in London, where his eloquence and talent for debate brought him to prominence in the Quaker movement. The appeal for support from Martha Simmonds in her dispute with other leading London Friends, and the ensuing risk of division, either coincided with or caused a breakdown which incapacitated him for a time. He was well enough to travel to Bristol in the summer of 1656, however, from where he set out to visit George Fox, then in prison in Launceston, who had been expressing concern that Nayler's ministry, and that of some of his associates, was becoming erratic. He was arrested as a vagabond, and imprisoned in Exeter. When Fox visited him there after his own release the meeting ended in an open breach.

Nayler was free by October 1656 and returned to Bristol in the company of a small group of Friends, including Martha Simmonds. They progressed via Glastonbury and Wells, and the ill-fated adventus into the city took place on 24 October. The group was arrested and Nayler and four others were sent to London to be examined by a committee of the Second Protectorate Parliament chaired by Thomas Bampfield. The subsequent trial of James Nayler was to a large extent political. Many MPs were suspicious of the religious freedom granted under the Protectorate and regarded Nayler's case as an example of the worst excesses of toleration. He was found guilty of 'horrid blasphemy' in December 1656. Despite Cromwell's call for leniency his punishment was brutal: put in the pillory, a hot iron was bored through his tongue and the letter B for Blasphemer was branded in his forehead. He was also flogged through the streets of London and Bristol. He remained in prison, with hard labour, until 1659, when the reconvened Rump Parliament declared an amnesty for Quaker prisoners. George Fox reluctantly agreed to a reconciliation and Nayler resumed preaching, though in broken health. Late in 1660 he set out for Yorkshire but was attacked and robbed near Huntingdon. He died on 21st October at the home of Thomas Parnell, a Quaker physician, in Kings Ripton, where he was buried in the former Quaker burial ground, now part of a private garden.

Martha Simmonds was born in 1624 in Somerset, where her father, George Calvert, was the vicar of Meare, near Glastonbury. She moved to London with her mother after her father's death, initially to live with her brother, Giles, who was a publisher established at the Black Spread-Eagle in St Pauls. Calvert in due course became the major publisher of Quaker writings, including her own and those of James Nayler. In 1655 she married Thomas Simmonds, a bookseller who had established himself at the Bull and Mouth with Calvert's help. By then Martha had become active in the Quaker movement, and was at the centre of a coterie of radicals which grew up around the Calvert and Simmonds households. She was already travelling, preaching, and disrupting meetings, and was imprisoned on more than one occasion. The summer of 1656 saw the development of an apocalyptic movement among a small group of Quakers, of which Martha was a leading figure. When she was reproached by Edward Burrough, Thomas Ellwood, Francis Howgill and other Quaker leaders, she appealed to Nayler. What followed is unclear. There seemed to be a danger of the movement fragmenting. During Nayler's breakdown Martha records that 'he lay at my house three daies'. When he left London to continue his ministry in Bristol Martha followed him. Early biographers represented Martha Simmonds as instrumental in the downfall of James Nayler, coming into his life 'like a whirlwind to cause havoc'. She was accused of witchcraft. One writer even suggests that Milton took Martha as the model for his figure of Eve. Although she was plainly an influence on Nayler, and took part in the adventus, it seems unrealistic to suggest that she was solely responsible for it. More recent biographers have recognised her as an articulate, courageous and engaging woman, and have drawn attention to her three religious texts, *When the Lord Jesus came to Jerusalem*, *A Lamentation for the Lost Sheep of the House of Israel*, and *O England Thy Time is Come*, all published by Giles Calvert. Accounts of the death of Martha Simmonds are contradictory. The burial records of the London and Middlesex Quarterly Meeting state that she died on 27 September 1665 and was buried the same day. Other sources record her death at sea in that year, en route to Maryland.

My Mephistopheles (243): See Isaiah 14: 12 for reference to his name and nature.